TWIST ON
TOFU

52 FRESH AND UNEXPECTED VEGETARIAN RECIPES

from Tofu Tacos and Quiche to Lasagna, Wings, Fries, and More

Corinne Trang

Photography by Kate Sears

Storey Publishing

To my daughter Colette,
who loves tofu prepared in any style

**The mission of Storey Publishing is to serve our customers by
publishing practical information that encourages
personal independence in harmony with the environment.**

Edited by Deanna F. Cook, Sarah Guare Slattery,
    and Lisa H. Hiley
Art direction and book design by Ash Austin
Text production by Slavica A. Walzl
Indexed by Andrea Chesman

Cover and interior photography by © Kate Sears,
    except back cover (author photo), courtesy of
    Corinne Trang
Additional interior photography by Mars Vilaubi
    © Storey Publishing, LLC, 4 t., 6, 8–11, 34, 38–39,
    51 (sauce); © Nadine Greeff/Stocksy, 12–13
Food styling by Liza Jernow

Text © 2022 by Corinne Trang

Storey books are available at special discounts when
purchased in bulk for premiums and sales promotions
as well as for fund-raising or educational use. Special
editions or book excerpts can also be created to spec-
ification. For details, please call 800-827-8673, or send
an email to sales@storey.com.

Storey Publishing
210 MASS MoCA Way
North Adams, MA 01247
storey.com

Printed in the United States, the interior by
    Versa Press and the cover by PC
10 9 8 7 6 5 4 3 2 1

Library of Congress Cataloging-in-Publication Data
    on file

Contents

VERSATILE AND DELICIOUS

Earthy and good for you, tofu is far from boring. It's incredibly flavorful—and absolutely misunderstood.

Tofu is a sponge. It absorbs all sorts of flavors, expanding ever so slightly while cooking and soaking up sauce, broth, or a medley of aromatics. It's versatile. It can be braised, grilled, steamed, poached, stir-fried, deep-fried, or pan-crisped and added to soups or salads and everything in between. Eat it cold, at room temperature, or hot, and enjoy it sweet or savory.

Originating and omnipresent in China, tofu has been consumed for more than two thousand years. It is derived from soybeans, which have been cultivated for about five thousand years and used to produce ancient and popular condiments such as soy sauce, tamari, hoisin, and miso, to name a few. Healthy and full of vitamins and minerals, soybeans belong to the legume family.

There are strong opinions about the benefits of eating tofu, but we only need to remember that the product has been consumed for millennia in China and other parts of Asia, where food is considered medicine and medicine, food. For generations, the peoples of Asia enjoyed a healthy lifestyle due to their particularly clean, mostly plant-based diet—that is, until Western fast food became part of the landscape. If we look back in time and start adopting the Asian diet, incorporating an abundance of vegetables, broth for cleansing, very small amounts of animal or seafood protein, and a bowl of rice or noodles, we may all be much healthier.

Tofu contains all nine essential amino acids and is a complete protein. It's gluten-free, 100 percent plant-based, and low in calories. More important, it is delicious, cholesterol-free, and a perfect alternative to meat and seafood. And eating it won't break the bank!

Growing up in an Asian family, I ate tofu, never questioning it. I feel lucky that way. I have enjoyed tofu in various forms, including braised in creamy coconut curry (page 87); stirred into miso soup (page 46); or simply poached, drizzled lightly with soy sauce and sesame oil, and garnished with julienned ginger and scallions (page 101).

I've also played with it in the kitchen, using it as an alternative protein in some of my favorite Western dishes. Take my word for it: Tofu makes a great replacement in familiar foods. Toss aside the burgers and throw some tofu steaks on the grill instead, and enjoy each bite with Asian barbecue sauce (page 41). If you're into Greek spinach pie but want a light alternative, crumble the tofu, skip the feta, and try a tofu and spinach empanada (page 69) instead. I also love to serve buttery, spicy tofu buffalo "wings" (page 18), a perfect finger food that will pleasantly surprise your guests at your next Super Bowl party.

Delightfully rich and filling, tofu is adaptable to any season or setting. Try the Asian-inspired tofu salad rolls with spicy tangy peanut (or almond) sauce (page 49) for your next picnic at the beach. Enjoy a bowl of steaming tofu chili (page 84) while getting cozy in front of the fireplace on a winter night. Slurp a wholesome tofu-mango lassi (page 109) for energy before your workout. Pack up a TLT&A sandwich (page 60) or Vietnamese banh mi with pickled vegetables (page 63) for lunch at the office. And if you're in a hurry, you can scoop and eat tofu right out of the container because it is a cooked product. It's not unusual for people to eat it plain.

By the time you've tried a handful of recipes, you'll love tofu—or at least like, appreciate, and understand it. My approach with any ingredient is always to give a little background, let the information settle in, then take the most popular foods on the market and reintroduce them with, in this case, tofu as the main ingredient. The ideas I share in the pages that follow are there for you to adapt and make your own, innovatively adding your own spin on tofu.

This book explores familiar, fuss-free, comfort foods from around the world. Filled with tips, the recipes are designed to please all palates, including those of tofu's toughest critics.

When you adopt a different perspective, have a little patience, and practice using tofu, you will open a door to endless possibilities in the kitchen. There are different types of tofu, each appropriate for specific uses and sometimes interchangeable. To be objective and develop a well-rounded opinion, you'll have to try tofu several times in all its facets—regular or silken, firm or soft! Get familiar with tofu by exploring Tofu 101 (page 6), a quick overview of the most popular and readily available tofu types and cooking techniques that will be key as you delve into the classic and contemporary everyday vegetarian recipes that follow. I promise, you're in for a treat.

HAPPY EATING!

TOFU 101

Regular or Silken?

For some time now, authentic, unseasoned Asian tofu (also called bean curd) has been readily available. In comparison, the seasoned types—part foreign and part familiar—are a newer Western invention meant to entice customers by making mealtimes easier. Using unseasoned tofu is best, as you are in control of the seasoning from start to finish, making it a healthier protein than those loaded with preservatives. As a rule, stick to plain tofu and have fun seasoning it yourself.

Tofu is sold submerged in water and packed in plastic containers, or, in the case of silken tofu, in hermetically sealed boxes, like the ones used for packaging single-serving juices.

To prepare regular tofu for cooking, simply pour off the water, then let the block sit on paper towels for 15 minutes to finish draining. There's no need to weight it after it is drained.

There are two basic types of plain tofu, each in a variety of densities.

REGULAR TOFU. Sold as a rectangular block or cake and submerged in water in plastic containers, this grainy or coarse tofu (sometimes referred to as Chinese tofu) can easily crumble, giving it a cottage cheese–like appearance. It is the most prevalent type of tofu sold in grocery stores. Regular tofu is available in soft, medium, firm, and extra-firm versions. The firmer it is, the richer in protein and the less likely it is to fall apart during cooking. The extra-firm version is ideal for stir-fries, while the soft version is best for braised dishes or soups.

SILKEN TOFU. Most often associated with Japanese cuisine, this tofu gets its name from its soft, custardlike texture. You can find it in most grocery stores, generally in hermetically sealed boxes, and Asian grocery stores even sell a variety of densities, including soft, firm, and extra-firm. Soft tofu resembles light-as-air custard, while extra-firm—still smooth in texture—is thick like Spanish flan. You can use the densities interchangeably in the recipes. There is also a lite version, which has fewer calories from fat. Silken tofu is perfect for making the classic and popular miso soup, as well as smoothies and dips.

CAN YOU USE THE DIFFERENT TYPES OF TOFU INTERCHANGEABLY? Yes, though sometimes with greater success than other times. If you don't care about texture and whether the tofu falls apart, use the texture you prefer. But if you enjoy appearance and variations on richness and textures, then use the tofu called for in each recipe.

Draining Tofu

Regular tofu is often drained to get rid of the water before cooking. Many recipes call for weighting the tofu to remove more water, but I prefer not to. I find that draining the water it is sold in is sufficient. Weighting the tofu causes the cake to release more water, rendering a dry and tough consistency when the tofu is cooked. When some of the water has been retained, the tofu is crispy on the outside and tender and moist on the inside when panfried, giving it a nice contrast.

To drain a cake of regular tofu, place a triple layer of paper towels on a large plate, set the tofu cake on top, then cover with another triple layer of paper towels. Drain for 15 minutes.

WHAT DOES TOFU TASTE LIKE?

Tofu does not taste like chicken! It also does not resemble cheese in any way, shape, or form. Tofu is a unique food. It is soybean derived and has its own earthy flavor. Trying to compare it to something else is not helpful. In general, if people like soy milk, they will like tofu. Even the most skeptical will find a recipe here they like, such as Vietnamese Tofu Banh Mi (page 63), Tex-Mex Tofu Chili (page 84), or Crispy Tofu Salad Rolls (also known as summer rolls; page 49), for instance.

Cutting Techniques

For best results, cut the regular tofu blocks or cakes into equal-size pieces. An easy way to do that is to cut them into halves, then halves, and halves again to the desired size, as illustrated below.

Thick-Cut "Fries," "Wings," and Nuggets

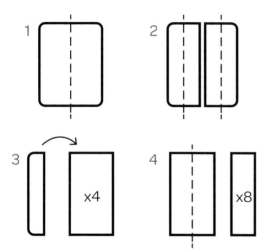

THICK-CUT "FRIES." Cut a block of tofu in half lengthwise, then cut each half lengthwise again. Flip the 4 thick, long rectangular slices flat onto your cutting board. Cut each rectangle in half lengthwise, so you have 8 long sticks that are about ¾ inch thick.

THICK-CUT "WINGS." Follow the directions above for thick-cut "fries," then cut each of the fries in half crosswise for a total of 16 "wings" about ¾ inch thick.

NUGGETS. Follow the instructions at left for thick-cut "wings," then cut each wing in half crosswise again for a total of 32 nuggets about ¾ inch thick.

Thin-Cut "Fries," "Wings," and Croutons

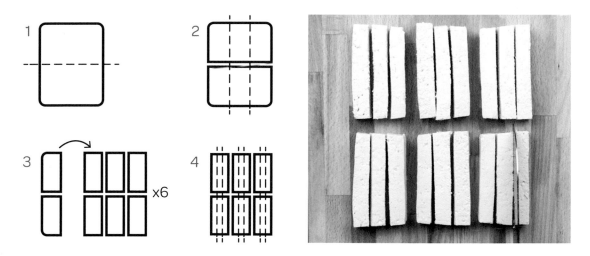

THIN-CUT "FRIES." Cut a block of tofu in half crosswise, then cut each half crosswise into thirds. Flip the 6 short rectangular slices flat onto your cutting board. Cut each rectangle lengthwise in thirds, so you have 18 long sticks about ½ inch thick.

THIN-CUT "WINGS." Follow the directions above for thin-cut "fries," then cut each of the fries in half crosswise for a total of 36 "wings" about ½ inch thick.

CROUTONS. Follow the instructions at left for thin-cut "wings," then cut each wing in half crosswise again for a total of 72 croutons about ½ inch thick.

Other Shapes

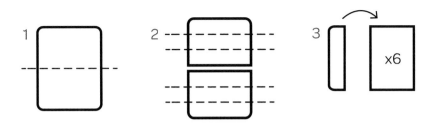

RECTANGLES. Cut a block of tofu in half crosswise. Now cut each half crosswise into 3 equally thick rectangles for a total of 6 "steaks" about ½ inch thick.

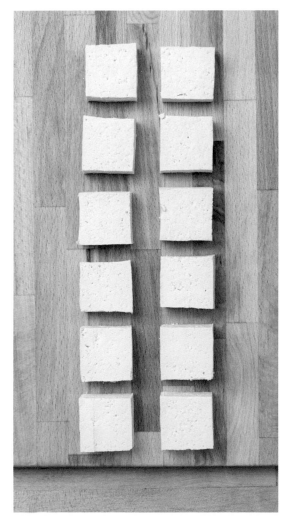 

SQUARES. Cut each rectangle in half cross-wise for a total of 12 squares about ½ inch thick.

TRIANGLES. Cut each square in half diago-nally for a total of 24 triangles about ½ inch thick.

Rectangles, squares, and triangles all work well for recipes that call for pan-crisping, panfrying, or grilling tofu.

RECIPES

Cooking is about letting loose, exploring possibilities, and, in this case, playing with tofu. The recipes in this book, all vegetarian or vegan, are your guide. I hope they entice you to get creative in the kitchen, tweaking them to your personal taste and folding in your favorite ingredients.

Though tofu is an Asian invention made from soybeans, you'll find that its spongelike ability to absorb flavor and be tasty in any number of combinations makes it very versatile. Whether you use the regular or silken type, and whether it's steamed, braised, fried, grilled, baked, stir-fried, or simply whipped, tofu is about to be the star in your kitchen.

1

Starters, Sides, or Small Plates

Finger foods or small bites are a perfect and delicate way to introduce tofu, especially to guests who have shied away from or may not be familiar with it. This chapter offers ideas for serving tofu in small portions and in ways that are familiar, such as tofu fries, hot wings, and even guacamole.

In no time, your guests will ask for more, so be sure to double up on quantities. Enjoy these bite-size morsels and the numerous textures, flavors, and colors they offer. No doubt there is something here to please every palate.

Thick-Cut Tofu French Fries
with Persillade

SERVES 4

Persillade, a combination of freshly chopped parsley and raw garlic, is a classic garnish in French cooking. Often sprinkled on raw, it has a sharp flavor. Here the garnish is flash-sautéed and scattered over the crispy fries for a milder yet flavorful and naturally sweeter version than its traditional form. Enjoy this recipe as an appetizer or snack with Dijon mustard for dipping, or enjoy the fries with a refreshing bed of salad greens for balance.

2   (14-ounce) containers **extra-firm regular tofu**, drained (page 7)

¼   cup **grapeseed** or **vegetable oil**

2   tablespoons **butter**

2   large **garlic cloves**, crushed and minced

6–8   **curly parsley sprigs**, leaves only, finely chopped

  Kosher salt and freshly ground **black pepper**

  Dijon mustard, for serving (optional)

  Mayonnaise, for serving (optional)

1   Cut each tofu cake in half lengthwise, then cut each half lengthwise again. Flip the rectangular slices flat onto your cutting board, then cut each rectangle in half lengthwise. You should have a total of 16 equal-size "fries" about ¾ inch thick (see thick-cut "fries," page 8).

2   Line a plate with paper towels. Pour the oil into a large nonstick pan over medium-high heat. Working in batches, add the tofu sticks in a single layer, making sure they stay separated, and panfry until golden brown all around, 1 to 2 minutes per side. Transfer to the paper towel–lined plate to drain, then move to a serving bowl.

3   Wipe the pan clean. Add the butter and let it melt over medium heat. Add the garlic and parsley and sauté until just warmed, about 20 seconds. Scatter over the tofu fries and season to taste with salt and pepper. Serve with Dijon (as is or combined with mayonnaise to taste) on the side for dipping, if desired.

TIP | Alternatively, make tofu nuggets by simply cutting the fries into smaller pieces, or into triangular pieces. You can make thinner fries, but do not cut them too thin as tofu can break easily.

Spicy Tofu Buffalo "Wings"

SERVES 4–8

Crispy on the outside and tender on the inside, tofu "wings" are best freshly made. Tossed in smoky, buttery chile-chipotle sauce, these will disappear fast. Serve them as a main course with a salad on the side, or as an appetizer at your next party.

FOR THE HOT SAUCE

- ⅓ cup **butter**, melted
- 3 **chipotle chiles** in adobo sauce, minced
- ¼ cup **adobo sauce**
- 1 tablespoon **distilled white vinegar**
- 1 teaspoon **garlic powder**
- **Kosher salt**

FOR THE BLUE CHEESE SAUCE

- ½ cup crumbled **blue cheese**
- ⅓ cup **heavy cream**
- Juice of ½ **lemon**
- 4–6 **chives**, chopped
- Freshly ground **black pepper**

FOR THE TOFU WINGS

- 2 (14-ounce) containers **extra-firm regular tofu**, drained (page 7)
- **Grapeseed** or **vegetable oil**, for panfrying
- 1 teaspoon **cornstarch**
- Chopped fresh **parsley**, for serving
- 4 **celery stalks**, strings removed, cut into ½- by 2-inch matchsticks, for serving

TIP | As an alternative to the delicious smoky, spicy butter sauce, you can make a classic buffalo sauce by substituting Louisiana Hot Sauce or Frank's RedHot for the minced chipotle chiles and the ¼ cup adobo sauce, using as much hot sauce as you like. This sauce keeps well, so feel free to make extra and refrigerate for future use.

1 To make the hot sauce, stir together the butter, chiles, adobo sauce, vinegar, and garlic powder in a medium bowl. Season to taste with salt.

2 To make the blue cheese sauce, stir together the blue cheese, cream, lemon juice, and chives in another small bowl. Season to taste with black pepper.

3 Cut each tofu cake in half lengthwise, then cut each half lengthwise again. Flip the rectangular slices flat onto your cutting board. Cut each rectangle in half lengthwise, then cut each of the sticks in half crosswise. You should have a total of 32 "wings" about ¾ inch thick (see thick-cut "wings," page 8).

4 Heat about ¼ inch of oil in a large deep non-stick skillet over medium-high heat.

5 Meanwhile, place the cornstarch in a large bowl and add the tofu, gently turning the pieces until coated evenly on all sides. Shake off the excess cornstarch.

6 Line a plate with paper towels. Working in batches, fry the tofu pieces in a single layer, making sure they stay separated. Cook until browned, 1 to 2 minutes per side. Drain the tofu on the paper towel–lined plate.

7 Transfer the fried tofu to a bowl and toss with half the hot sauce; add more if you like a spicier result. Transfer the tofu to a platter, garnish with parsley, and serve with the blue cheese sauce and celery sticks on the side.

Crispy Soy-Sesame Tofu Nuggets

SERVES 4–8

Tofu crisps easily. Sometimes you can coat it with tapioca starch or cornstarch for a little extra crunch. Feel free to experiment. Once crispy, tofu can be tossed in all sorts of sauces you might come up with, such as this Asian-inspired soy-sesame-ginger sauce. The sauce makes these tofu nuggets tasty served on a bed of greens (see the kale salad on page 48). You can also serve these nuggets as an appetizer or as a snack.

2   (14-ounce) containers **extra-firm regular tofu**, drained (page 7)

⅓   cup **soy sauce**

1   tablespoon **toasted sesame oil**

2   tablespoons **maple syrup**

1   (1-inch) piece fresh **ginger**, peeled and grated

1   **scallion**, root end and tough green top trimmed, white and green parts minced

1   medium **garlic clove**, grated

     Grapeseed or **vegetable oil**, for panfrying

¼   cup **tapioca starch** or **cornstarch**

     Toasted sesame seeds, for garnish

1 Cut each tofu cake in half lengthwise, then cut each half lengthwise again. Flip the rectangular slices flat onto your cutting board, then cut each rectangle in half lengthwise to make 16 sticks total. Cut each stick in half crosswise, then halve crosswise again. You should have a total of 64 nuggets (see page 8).

2 For the sauce, stir together the soy sauce, sesame oil, maple syrup, ginger, scallion, and garlic in a small bowl. Set aside.

3 Heat about ¼ inch of grapeseed oil in a large deep nonstick skillet over medium-high heat.

4 Meanwhile, place the tapioca starch in a large bowl and add the tofu pieces, gently turning them until coated evenly on all sides. Shake off the excess starch.

5 Line a plate with paper towels. Working in batches, fry the pieces in a single layer, making sure they stay separated. Cook until browned, 1 to 2 minutes per side. Drain the tofu on the paper towel–lined plate.

6 Transfer the fried tofu to a bowl and toss with 2 tablespoons of sauce. (Serve the remaining sauce on the side for dipping.) Garnish the seasoned tofu lightly with toasted sesame seeds.

Roasted Tofu-Stuffed Mushrooms
with Cheese

SERVES 4

Portobello mushrooms are sturdy and meaty, and great for stuffing with tofu. Topped with cheese and roasted until gooey and golden, these treats are perfect served alongside a refreshing salad for a balanced meal. Use a cheese that has good flavor yet will not mask the delicate flavor of tofu.

8 large **portobello mushroom caps**, gills scraped out

4 tablespoons **olive oil**

1 medium **onion**, finely chopped

2 large **garlic cloves**, minced

1 (14-ounce) container **extra-firm regular tofu**, drained (page 7) and crumbled (see Notes)

1 small head **broccoli**, florets shaved into a powder (about 1 cup; see Notes)

2 **thyme sprigs**, leaves only

Kosher salt and freshly ground **black pepper**

1½ cups grated **cheddar cheese** or 16 thin slices **smoked mozzarella**

TIPS | Firm tofu will crumble easily with a fork or with your hands.

To "shave" the broccoli head, simply slice close to the edges of the florets with a knife. This will create a fine green dust.

1 Preheat the oven to 400°F (200°C). Line a baking pan with parchment paper and set it aside.

2 Rub the mushrooms with 2 tablespoons of the oil.

3 Heat the remaining 2 tablespoons oil in a medium pan over medium heat. Add the onion and garlic and, stirring occasionally, sauté until golden, about 10 minutes. Transfer to a large mixing bowl. Add the tofu, broccoli, and thyme, and toss to combine. Season to taste with salt and pepper.

4 Divide the tofu mixture into 8 equal portions and use to stuff each mushroom cap. Place the caps stuffing side up on the parchment paper–lined baking pan. Top each stuffed mushroom with cheese. Bake until golden and the cheese bubbles, 15 to 20 minutes.

Tofu, Pea, and Mushroom Dumplings

SERVES 4–6

Round or square, dumpling wrappers are available in the refrigerated section of the produce aisle in most supermarkets. The folding technique never has to be complicated. In fact, you can simply fold the wrapper in half over the filling to make a rectangular or half-moon shape. It's fast and easy and will give you a good amount of crispness.

To keep the filling-to-wrapper ratio balanced, be sure not to overstuff these bite-size morsels. Boiling the dumplings makes for a delicate and relatively light meal, while pot stickers (panfried dumplings) offer a richer bite.

FOR THE DIPPING SAUCE

- ½ cup **soy sauce**
- ⅓ cup **rice vinegar**
- 1 tablespoon **toasted sesame oil**
- 1 (1½-inch) piece fresh **ginger**, finely grated
- 1 **scallion**, root end and tough green top trimmed, white and green parts minced
- 1–2 teaspoons **sambal oelek** (optional)

FOR THE DUMPLINGS

- 1 (14-ounce) container **firm** or **extra-firm regular tofu**, drained (page 7) and crumbled
- 8 dried **shiitake mushrooms**, soaked in water until soft, stems removed, and caps finely chopped
- ½ cup fresh or thawed frozen **peas**
- 1 **scallion**, root end and tough green top trimmed, white and green parts minced
- 1 tablespoon grated fresh **ginger**
- 2 tablespoons **soy sauce**
- 2 teaspoons **toasted sesame oil**
- 2 teaspoons **cornstarch**

  Freshly ground **black pepper**
- 64 **wonton wrappers**
- ½ loosely packed cup **cilantro leaves**, for garnish

  Grapeseed or **vegetable oil**, for panfrying (optional)

Recipe continues on next page

TOFU, PEA, AND MUSHROOM DUMPLINGS,
continued

1 To make the dipping sauce, stir together the soy sauce, rice vinegar, sesame oil, ginger, scallion, and sambal oelek (if using) in a small bowl. Set aside.

2 To make the dumplings, mix together the tofu, mushrooms, peas, scallion, ginger, soy sauce, sesame oil, and cornstarch in a large bowl. Season to taste with pepper.

3 Fill a small bowl with water. Place a heaping teaspoon of the tofu mixture in the center of a wonton wrapper. Dip your fingertip in the water and run it across the inside edge of the wrapper, around the filling. Fold the wrapper in half, squeezing air out while securing the filling. Repeat this step with the remaining wrappers and filling, placing the dumplings on a plate in a single layer and separated.

4 **TO BOIL THE DUMPLINGS,** bring a pot of water to a boil over high heat. Working in batches if necessary, add the dumplings and cook until they come up to the surface, 2 to 3 minutes. Using a slotted spoon, transfer an equal amount of cooked dumplings to individual bowls. Serve drizzled with dipping sauce and topped with some cilantro.

TO PANFRY THE DUMPLINGS, line a plate with paper towels. Add ¼ cup grapeseed oil and ¼ cup water in a large nonstick skillet with a lid over medium heat. Working in batches, place as many dumplings as can fit in a single layer, without them touching. Cover, increase the heat to medium-high, and cook until the water has evaporated completely and the underside of each dumpling is golden brown. (Do not flip. The underside should be fried while the top side should be steamed, providing a contrast in color and texture.) Transfer to the paper towel–lined plate to drain.

Repeat with the remaining batches, replenishing the pan with only water for the second batch, with oil and water for the third batch, and again with only water for the fourth batch, and so on as needed. Garnish with cilantro and serve with dipping sauce on the side.

Tofu-Avocado Toast
with Ginger-Scallion-Salt Paste

SERVES 4

When it comes to avocado toast, variations abound. This version has a ginger-scallion-salt paste, a classic condiment in Chinese Hakka cuisine that is often served with poached or steamed chicken. It is also a delicious topping for this whipped tofu–avocado toast. Though you can grab any bread, a wholesome multigrain type is highly recommended as a base, for the rich, nutty note it adds to each bite.

1 (2-inch) piece fresh **ginger**, peeled and finely grated

6 **scallions**, root ends and tough green tops trimmed, white and green parts minced

3 tablespoons **grapeseed** or **vegetable oil**

1 teaspoon **kosher salt**

2 ripe **Hass avocados**, halved, pitted, and peeled

½ (12-ounce) container **silken tofu**

Juice of 1 **lime**

Pinch of **cayenne pepper** (optional)

6 slices **whole-grain bread**, toasted and halved diagonally

1 Mix together the ginger, scallions, oil, and salt in a small bowl to form a paste.

2 Place the avocados, tofu, lime juice, and cayenne (if using) in a food processor. Process until smooth.

3 Take the toast points and put an equal amount of the avocado-tofu mixture in the center of each. Using a knife blade or pastry knife, shape the topping from the center down to the sides, building a mound in the center. Top each piece with a dollop of the salty herb paste and serve.

TIPS | Refrain from seasoning the spread—the ginger-scallion-salt paste provides a good sharp amount.

Turn this delicious avocado toast into a roll by using scallion flatbreads (see page 33).

Tofu Tacos

SERVES 4 (MAKES 12 TACOS)

Taco night pleases just about anyone at the table. An easy way to warm the tortillas is to place them in a bowl, cover the bowl with plastic wrap, and microwave for 30 seconds. Alternatively, soften them in a pan over medium to low heat. The tofu can be sautéed, panfried, or grilled. The texture is entirely up to you.

1	(14-ounce) container **firm** or **extra-firm regular tofu**, drained (page 7)
½	cup **distilled white vinegar**
1	tablespoon **sugar**
2	teaspoons **kosher salt**, plus more for seasoning
¼	head **red cabbage**, finely julienned
2	teaspoons **dried oregano**
1	teaspoon **smoked paprika**
½	teaspoon **cumin powder**
3	tablespoons **grapeseed** or **vegetable oil**
12	8-inch **tortillas**, corn, plain, or flavored
4–6	**romaine** or **iceberg lettuce leaves**, finely julienned
1	small **onion** or large **shallot**, minced
2	large ripe **avocados**, halved, pitted, peeled, and thinly sliced lengthwise
2	**limes**, each cut crosswise into 8 wedges, exposing all sections
1	small bunch **cilantro**, leaves only
	Pickled jalapeños
	Freshly ground **black pepper**

1   Cut the tofu cake in half lengthwise, then cut each half lengthwise again. Flip the 4 rectangular slices flat onto your cutting board, then cut each rectangle in half lengthwise to make 8 sticks. Cut each stick in half crosswise, then halve crosswise again. You should have 32 nuggets (see page 8).

2   Whisk together the vinegar, sugar, and salt in a large mixing bowl until the granules are completely dissolved. Add the cabbage and toss until well coated. Set aside, tossing occasionally as the cabbage wilts.

3   Stir together the oregano, paprika, and cumin in a small bowl. Sprinkle both sides of the tofu squares with this spice mixture.

4   Heat the oil in a nonstick pan over medium heat. Add the tofu nuggets and cook until light golden, about 1 minute per side.

5   Drain the cabbage and transfer to a serving bowl. Alongside this bowl set the tortillas, lettuce, onion, avocado, lime wedges, cilantro, and jalapeños, each in their own dish. For a do-it-yourself approach, use any of the ingredients for each taco, incorporating the tofu into the mix. Alternatively, use them all: Take a tortilla, add some lettuce and cabbage, top with 3 tofu pieces, and garnish with onion, avocado, cilantro, and jalapeño. Add a squeeze of lime and season to taste with salt and pepper.

Cold Citrus-Soy Tofu

· SERVES 4

This is one dish you can easily make with any type of tofu—from firm to soft and regular to silken. Enjoy this tofu dish as an appetizer, a small plate, or as part of a main course any time of the year, at room temperature or lightly chilled.

1 (12-ounce) container **firm silken tofu**

2 tablespoons **soy sauce**

1 tablespoon fresh-squeezed **lemon juice**

2 teaspoons **toasted sesame oil**

½ teaspoon **agave nectar**

1 **scallion**, root end and tough green top trimmed, white and green parts thinly sliced into rounds

1 tablespoon **pickled ginger**, squeezed gently

1 Cut the tofu cake in half crosswise, then cut each half crosswise into 3 equally thick rectangles for a total of 6 rectangles. Flip each rectangle flat onto your cutting board. Cut each in half crosswise for a total of 12 squares about ½ inch thick (see page 11).

2 Stir together the soy sauce, lemon juice, oil, and agave nectar in a small bowl until well combined.

3 Overlap the tofu pieces on a small dish. Drizzle the soy sauce mixture over them and scatter the scallion and ginger on top. Serve immediately.

Tofu Satay

SERVES 4

Popular in Indonesia and Malaysia, satay is a dish of spice-marinated cubed, skewered, and grilled meat. Here the dish is adapted with readily available ingredients and extra-firm tofu, then served with peanut sauce for dipping. Satay is excellent as an appetizer or party food, or you can enjoy it with rice and pickled vegetables on the side for a complete meal.

FOR THE SATAY

- 2 (14-ounce) containers **extra-firm regular tofu**, drained (page 7)
- ½ cup **grapeseed** or **vegetable oil**
- 2 small **shallots**, finely grated
- 2 large **garlic cloves**, finely grated
- 1 tablespoon **agave nectar**
- 1 tablespoon **ground coriander**
- 1 teaspoon **turmeric powder**
- 1 teaspoon **cayenne pepper**

FOR THE PEANUT SAUCE

- Juice of 1 **lemon** or **lime**
- ⅓ cup pure **peanut butter** or **almond butter** (see Note)
- ½ cup lite **coconut milk** or **water**
- ¼ cup **hoisin sauce**
- 2 teaspoons **agave nectar**
- 1–2 teaspoons **Sriracha sauce** or **sambal oelek**

TIP | For the best and tastiest results, use 100 percent pure roasted peanut or almond butter with zero additives.

1 If you will be cooking the satay on an outdoor grill, soak four 10- to 15-inch bamboo skewers in water for 20 minutes. Alternatively, you can cook the tofu cubes by themselves and then skewer them for presentation.

2 To make the satay, cut each block of tofu into 8 equal cubes, for a total of 16 cubes. Stir together ¼ cup plus 2 tablespoons of the oil with the shallots, garlic, agave nectar, coriander, turmeric, and cayenne in a medium baking dish. Spread the paste in the dish, then add the tofu, turning each cube on all sides to coat evenly. Slide 4 tofu cubes onto each skewer (if using).

3 Heat the remaining 2 tablespoons oil in a large nonstick pan or grill pan over medium heat. When the oil starts to smoke, add the tofu skewers and cook until the first side is golden and crispy, about 1 minute. Flip to the next side and crisp for 1 minute, and repeat the flipping and crisping until the cubes are a rich golden brown on all sides, about 6 minutes total.

4 To make the peanut sauce, combine the lemon juice, peanut (or almond) butter, coconut milk, hoisin, agave nectar, and Sriracha in a medium bowl.

5 Serve the tofu with the peanut sauce on the side for dipping.

Whipped Tofu Guacamole
with Scallion Flatbreads

SERVES 4

This whipped silken tofu and avocado guacamole is extremely simple to make. Be sure to use ripe Hass avocados for the best results. These come from Mexico and are generally creamy and sweet. Fresh lemon juice and kosher salt will keep the color bright green. The freshly made scallion flatbreads can be torn or cut into triangles for dipping.

FOR THE GUACAMOLE

1   (12-ounce) container **silken tofu**

2   ripe **Hass avocados**, halved, pitted, and peeled (see Tip)

1   tablespoon **shiro miso (white miso)**

    Juice of 1 **lemon**

    Kosher salt

1–2   teaspoons **Sriracha sauce** (optional)

FOR THE FLATBREADS

1½   cups **all-purpose flour**, plus more for kneading

1½   teaspoons **baking powder**

¾   cup cold or room-temperature **water**

    Toasted sesame oil

    Kosher salt

8   **scallions**, root ends and tough green tops trimmed, white and green parts thinly sliced

    Grapeseed or **vegetable oil** for cooking, about 1 tablespoon of oil per flatbread

TIP | Look for smooth-skinned (rather than bumpy) green avocados. Ripen them on your kitchen counter. After 3 days, they will start to give to the touch. In 4 to 5 days, they are perfectly ripened. Refrigerate them to stop the ripening process. They should be bright yellowish green and buttery when you cut them open.

1 To make the guacamole, place the tofu, avocados, miso, and lemon juice in a food processor. Season to taste with salt and add the Sriracha, if and as desired. Process until smooth and transfer to a serving bowl. Cover with plastic wrap and refrigerate until 15 minutes prior to serving.

2 To make the flatbreads, use a fork to stir together the flour and baking powder in a medium bowl. Make a well in the center and add the water. Starting in the center and working outward, stir together the flour and water until they form a ball of dough. Turn out onto a floured work surface and knead for 5 minutes. Cover with plastic wrap and let rest for 20 minutes.

Recipe continues on next page

WHIPPED TOFU GUACAMOLE,
continued

3 Flour a clean work surface and turn out the dough. Knead it a few times, then roll it into a thick rope and cut it into 8 equal pieces. Working with one piece at a time, roll the dough between your hands to form a smooth ball, then flatten it on the work surface.

Using a pin, roll each piece into a thin oval or rectangle about 4 by 8 inches long (photo 3a). Brush some sesame oil across the top, sprinkle lightly with salt, and scatter generously with scallions (photo 3b).

Roll the dough tightly into a cigar, securing the scallions (photo 3c). Form the cigar into a coil (photo 3d) and place it under plastic wrap. Repeat with the remaining dough pieces until you have 8 coils. Keep under plastic wrap and let rest for 10 minutes.

4 Flour the work surface again and roll each piece of dough into a very thin disk (photo 4).

5 Generously oil a nonstick skillet and heat over medium heat. When the pan is hot, add one disk and cook until golden spots develop on each side, 3 to 5 minutes total, flipping once or twice. Cook the remaining flatbreads and serve them, freshly torn or sliced into thin triangles, with the guacamole.

Steamed Chile-Ginger Tofu

SERVES 4

I often prefer simple preparations over complex ones, using either basic ingredients or minimal spicing. This steamed tofu dish couldn't be easier to make. Served over rice and with stir-fried greens, this can be part of a wholesome, high-protein, tasty meal for many.

2 tablespoons **grapeseed** or **vegetable oil**

3 **scallions**, root ends and tough green tops trimmed, white and green parts chopped

1 (2-inch) piece fresh **ginger**, peeled and finely julienned

2 large **garlic cloves**, minced

1 red **Thai chile** or **jalapeño**, stem and seeds removed, thinly sliced

1 bunch **cilantro**, stems trimmed lightly, chopped

⅓ cup **soy sauce**

¼ cup **rice vinegar**

1 tablespoon **toasted sesame oil**

2 (12-ounce) containers **silken tofu**

2 **lettuce leaves**

1 Heat the grapeseed oil in a saucepan over high heat. Add the scallions, ginger, and garlic, and stir-fry until golden, 2 to 3 minutes. Add the chile and stir-fry until golden, about 1 minute. Stir in the cilantro and cook until wilted, about 1 minute. Transfer the mixture to a heatproof bowl and stir in the soy sauce, vinegar, and sesame oil.

2 Halve each tofu cake crosswise. Pour water into a wok outfitted with a bamboo steamer or the bottom of a double boiler. Line the top insert with the lettuce and place the 4 pieces of tofu on top. Cover and bring to a boil over high heat. Steam for 5 minutes.

3 Using a spatula, carefully transfer each tofu piece to an individual small bowl or soup plate. Spoon some of the stir-fried herbs and sauce over each portion and serve.

Tofu Veggie Seaweed Rolls

MAKES 12 ROLLS

These short-grain rice and nori seaweed rolls can be filled with all sorts of vegetables. These rolls tend to be on the large side, much like Korean-style kimbap rolls, but feel free to experiment and make different-size rolls. Use the full sheet of nori to make kimbap, or cut off one-third of the sheet, horizontally, to make Japanese-style maki. You can also quarter the nori sheet and make hand rolls (see Tip, page 39).

2 (14-ounce) containers **firm regular tofu**, drained (page 7)

4 cups freshly cooked **sushi rice**

¼ cup seasoned **rice vinegar**

2 tablespoons **grapeseed** or **vegetable oil**

8 fresh **shiitake mushrooms**, stems removed and caps julienned

1 large **carrot**, peeled and cut into 2-inch-long matchsticks

1 pound (16 ounces) **baby spinach** leaves

1 teaspoon **toasted sesame oil**

12 **nori sheets**

Toasted sesame seeds, for garnish

Pickled ginger, for serving

Soy sauce, for serving

Wasabi, for serving

1 Cut each tofu cake in half crosswise, then cut each half crosswise into thirds. Flip the short rectangular slices flat onto your cutting board, then cut each rectangle lengthwise into thirds. You should have a total of 36 equal-size "fries" about ½ inch thick (see thin-cut "fries," page 9).

2 Add the warm rice to a large baking dish, sprinkle with the vinegar, then mix and spread the rice thoroughly. Fan to cool. Divide into 12 equal portions.

3 Meanwhile, heat the grapeseed oil in a medium pan over high heat, then add the mushrooms and stir-fry until just wilted, 5 to 10 minutes. Remove from the heat.

4 Fill a small pot with salted water and bring to a boil over high heat. Add the carrot matchsticks and blanch for 1 minute. Using a slotted spoon, transfer the matchsticks to a bowl to cool. Add the spinach to the same water and blanch for 10 seconds. With a slotted spoon, transfer the spinach to a second bowl to cool. When the spinach is cool enough to handle, gently squeeze any water out of it. Drizzle the sesame oil over the spinach.

Recipe continues on next page

TOFU VEGGIE SEAWEED ROLLS,
continued

5 Place a small bowl of water on your clean work surface. Lay out one sheet of nori. Wet your working hand and grab a portion of rice. Starting with the side closest to you, thinly and evenly spread the rice horizontally, all the way to the edges, over two-thirds of the nori's surface (photo 5a). On the side closest to you, and about 1 inch in, create a thin horizontal strip of mushroom, carrot, spinach, and 2 pieces of tofu (photo 5b). Fold the nori over the ingredients and, holding it tight, keep rolling it into a thick cigar, rolling all the way to the end (photo 5c). Set aside and repeat with the remaining ingredients until you have 12 rolls.

6 Slice each roll crosswise into 8 pieces. Sprinkle with sesame seeds and serve with pickled ginger and soy sauce and wasabi for dipping.

TIP | Alternatively, to make hand rolls, quarter a sheet of nori, spreading each piece with about 3 tablespoons of rice. Add some mushroom, carrot, and spinach, then top with 1 tofu stick. Roll and shape into a cone. Enjoy with soy sauce spiced with wasabi on the side.

Tofu in Black Bean Sauce

SERVES 4

Chinese black bean and garlic sauce is a condiment easily found in supermarkets, and it's good to have on hand for a quick meal. In this recipe, the basic sauce is generously infused with ginger, rice wine, and extra garlic. A classic dish, tofu with black bean and garlic sauce can be served as is, over rice, or tossed with wheat noodles.

2 (14-ounce) containers **firm** or **extra-firm regular tofu**, drained (page 7)

¼ cup **grapeseed** or **vegetable oil**

2 large **garlic cloves**, thinly sliced

1 (2-inch) piece fresh **ginger**, peeled and finely julienned

2 red **Thai chiles**, stems and seeds removed, finely sliced

⅓ cup **Chinese black bean and garlic sauce**

½ cup **sake**

Pinch of **sugar**

1 teaspoon **cornstarch** mixed with 1 tablespoon **water**

½ cup **cilantro**, leaves only, for garnish

1 Cut each tofu cake in half lengthwise, then cut each half lengthwise again. Flip the rectangular slices flat onto your cutting board, then cut each rectangle in half lengthwise to make 16 sticks total. Cut each stick in half crosswise, then halve crosswise again. You should have a total of 64 nuggets (see page 8).

2 Heat 2 tablespoons of the oil in a small saucepan over high heat. Add the garlic and ginger and sauté until golden, about 3 minutes. Reduce the heat to medium-low and add the chiles, black bean and garlic sauce, sake, and sugar. Stir in the cornstarch slurry and cook until slightly thickened, about 2 minutes. Remove from the heat.

3 Heat the remaining 2 tablespoons oil in a large nonstick skillet over medium heat. Add the tofu cubes and panfry, turning the cubes until lightly golden on all sides, 8 to 10 minutes. Add the black bean sauce, toss for 1 minute, transfer to a serving dish, and garnish with the cilantro.

TIPS | If you can't find fresh Thai chiles, use 2 jalapeños or one-third of a Scotch bonnet chile for a spicy yet slightly different taste.

Though this recipe calls for regular firm or extra-firm tofu, you can easily use regular soft tofu for a different appearance and texture. In general, the softer the tofu, the lighter it is and the more it breaks apart.

Grilled Spicy Sweet BBQ Tofu

SERVES 4

Barbecue sauce is a favorite everywhere, and this Asian-inspired version is infused with Chinese five-spice powder and hoisin sauce, Korean gochujang (chile bean paste), and Japanese mirin (sweet sake). Delicious with tofu cooked any style, this sticky sweet-and-spicy sauce is particularly well suited to this grilled, thick-cut, ever-so-slightly charred version.

½   cup **sake**

⅓   cup **hoisin sauce**

⅓   cup **rice vinegar**

¼   cup **mirin**

¼   cup **gochujang**

2   tablespoons **soy sauce**

2   teaspoons **five-spice powder**

1   tablespoon **sugar**

2   (14-ounce) containers **extra-firm regular tofu**, drained (page 7)

2   tablespoons **grapeseed** or **vegetable oil**

2   **scallions**, root ends and tough green tops trimmed, white and green parts finely sliced, for garnish

Toasted sesame seeds, for garnish

1 Whisk together the sake, hoisin, vinegar, mirin, gochujang, soy sauce, five-spice powder, and sugar in a small saucepan over medium to low heat until well combined. Cook until reduced and thickened to the consistency of loose custard (that is, not too thick and not too thin), about 15 minutes. Remove from the heat and set aside to cool.

2 Cut each tofu cake in half crosswise, then cut each half crosswise into 3 equally thick rectangles. You should have a total of 12 rectangles about ½ inch thick (see page 10).

3 Heat the oil in a grill pan over high heat. Add the tofu "steaks" and grill until golden brown on both sides, about 5 minutes total. Place 3 steaks each on four individual plates, drizzle with the barbecue sauce to taste, and garnish with scallions and a light sprinkling of sesame seeds.

TIP | Try this recipe with pan-crisped tofu triangles (see page 11).

Grilled Tofu
with Kale Pesto

SERVES 4

1 large head **garlic**

⅓–½ cup **olive oil**, plus more for greasing

6 large **curly kale leaves**, ribs removed

1 cup grated **Grana Padano cheese**, plus more as needed

1 cup plain dry-roasted **walnut pieces**

½ bunch **basil**, leaves only

Kosher salt and freshly ground **black pepper**

2 (14-ounce) containers **soft**, **firm**, or **extra-firm regular tofu**, drained (page 7)

Red pepper flakes, for garnish (optional)

TIP | Make the pesto ahead of time; it won't change color, unlike the classic basil version, which darkens. Pesto will keep well refrigerated for up to 1 week or frozen for up to 3 months. For this grilled tofu dish, ¼ to ⅓ cup of pesto is plenty; the recipe makes about 2½ cups, though it all depends on the size of the kale leaves.

I love a good pesto. This kale version with roasted garlic and walnuts is hearty and retains its attractive bright green color. Readily available Grana Padano is the cheese base. I find it sweeter and milder than Parmesan and more complementary to tofu as a result.

1 Preheat the oven to 400°F (200°C).

2 Slice off the very top of the garlic head, just enough to reveal the cloves. Place the head cut side up on a piece of aluminum foil large enough to envelop it. Drizzle with 1 teaspoon of the oil and wrap to secure. Place on a baking pan and roast for about 40 minutes, until tender and fragrant.

3 With a butter knife, remove the roasted cloves from the skin and transfer to a food processor. Add the kale, cheese, walnuts, and basil. With the processor running, gradually stream in ⅓ cup of the oil. Add more oil as needed to achieve the desired consistency. Season to taste with salt and black pepper.

4 Cut each tofu cake in half crosswise, then cut each half crosswise into 3 equally thick rectangles. Flip each rectangle flat onto your cutting board. Cut each in half crosswise. You should have a total of 24 squares about ½ inch thick (see page 11).

5 Oil a nonstick grill pan and place over medium heat. Grill the tofu squares until crispy on both sides, about 5 minutes total. Divide among four serving plates, garnishing each piece with a dollop of pesto and a light sprinkling of red pepper flakes, if desired.

2
Soups and Salads

The delicious, wholesome seasonal soups and salads in this section provide a touch of comforting warmth as well as healthy, cooling refreshment. Tofu is often added to soup in Asia. It's filling, absorbs all sorts of flavors, and stays hot. One of the most well-known soups using pillowy-soft silken tofu, for example, is miso soup, a Japanese restaurant favorite. Tofu is adaptable and also can be crisped like croutons and added as a topping to all sorts of salads.

Tofu, Pea, and Mushroom Miso Soup

SERVES 4

This soup takes about five minutes to make: the time it takes to bring water to a boil. It's that easy. On the most basic level, it's a miso soup base with silken tofu, some seaweed, and scallions. That's the way it is served in typical Japanese sushi restaurants. However, you can add all sorts of ingredients—such as noodles, spinach, and other types of vegetables—to make it a more filling yet still light soup. Let the weather inspire what you put in the pot!

1 quart **water**

⅓ cup **shiro miso (white miso)**

6 medium fresh **shiitake mushrooms**, stems removed and caps julienned

½ cup fresh or frozen **peas**

1 (12-ounce) container **silken tofu**

1 tablespoon **wakame seaweed**, rehydrated in water, drained, and chopped

1 **scallion**, root end and tough green top trimmed, white and green parts thinly sliced into rounds, for garnish

1 tablespoon **toasted sesame oil**, for garnish (optional)

2 teaspoons finely grated fresh **ginger**, for garnish (optional)

Toasted sesame seeds, for garnish (optional)

Shichimi togarashi powder, for garnish (optional)

1 Bring the water to a boil in a medium stockpot over high heat. Reduce the heat to medium and whisk in the miso until diluted. Add the mushrooms and peas and cook until heated through, about 5 minutes.

2 Cut the tofu cake in half lengthwise, then cut each half lengthwise again. Flip the 4 rectangular slices flat onto your cutting board, then cut each rectangle in half lengthwise to make 8 sticks. Cut each stick in half crosswise, then halve crosswise again. You should have 32 nuggets (see page 8).

3 Divide the tofu and wakame among four individual soup bowls. Pour an equal amount of soup, with mushrooms and peas, into each bowl. Top each serving with scallions. If desired, garnish each bowl with some sesame oil, ginger, and sesame seeds and a pinch or two of shichimi togarashi.

Kale and Crispy Soy-Sesame Tofu Nugget Salad

SERVES 4

Kale is delicious raw. Use any type for this salad, including Tuscan, Red Russian, and curly kale. The latter will give you the most volume. I like to mix them up for a variety of textures and colors. The Japanese-inspired dressing will complement these hearty leaves as well as the crouton topping.

12   large **kale leaves**, ribs removed and leaves julienned, chopped, or torn (see Tips)

    Pinch of **kosher salt**

⅓   cup plus 1 teaspoon **grapeseed** or **vegetable oil**

    Juice of 1 **lemon**

1   tablespoon **shiro miso (white miso)**

2   teaspoons **toasted sesame oil**

1   teaspoon **Sriracha sauce**

1   (1-inch) piece fresh **ginger**, peeled and finely grated

1   **scallion**, root end and tough green top trimmed, white and green parts minced

    Crispy Soy-Sesame Tofu Nuggets (page 20)

1   Toss together the kale, salt, and 1 teaspoon grapeseed oil in a large bowl. Gently massage the leaves for a minute to tenderize them.

2   Whisk together the lemon juice and miso in a small bowl until smooth. Add the sesame oil, Sriracha, and the remaining ⅓ cup grapeseed oil, and whisk again. Stir in the ginger and scallion, then pour the dressing over the kale. Toss well and garnish with tofu nuggets.

TIPS | After removing the ribs, julienne Tuscan kale leaves, chop curly kale leaves, and tear Red Russian kale leaves.

Not all lemons are created equal in terms of tanginess and the amount of juice you get. Adjust the dressing by adding more lemon or oil, depending on your personal preference.

Crispy Tofu Salad Rolls

SERVES 4 (MAKES 16 ROLLS)

Known as fresh spring rolls or summer rolls in the West, Vietnamese goi cuon, or "salad rolls," are the inspiration for this dish. Made with a mixture of cooked and raw ingredients, they are balanced and delicious dipped in peanut (or almond) sauce. Serve these freshly made. Do not refrigerate, as the rice paper hardens when cold.

FOR THE SALAD ROLLS

2 (14-ounce) containers **extra-firm regular tofu**, drained (page 7)

⅓ cup **grapeseed** or **vegetable oil**

16 **Boston, Bibb,** or **oak leaf lettuce leaves**, ribs discarded

1 small **carrot**, peeled and finely julienned into 2-inch-long pieces

½ **English cucumber**, peeled and julienned into 2-inch-long pieces

32 large **mint leaves**

2 **scallions**, root ends and tough green tops trimmed, white and green parts julienned into 2-inch-long pieces

3 ounces **rice vermicelli**, soaked in water

12 (8- to 10-inch) **rice papers**

FOR THE PEANUT SAUCE

⅓ cup pure **peanut butter** or **almond butter**

½ cup lite **coconut milk** or **water**

¼ cup **hoisin sauce**

Juice of 1 **lemon** or **lime**

2 teaspoons **agave nectar**

1–2 teaspoons **Sriracha sauce** or **sambal oelek**

1 To make the salad rolls, cut each tofu cake in half lengthwise, then cut each half lengthwise again. Flip the rectangular slices flat onto your cutting board, then cut each rectangle in half lengthwise. You should have a total of 16 equal-size "fries" about ¾ inch thick (see thick-cut "fries," page 8).

2 Line a plate with paper towels. Heat half of the oil in a large nonstick pan over medium heat. Add half of the tofu sticks and panfry until golden brown all around, 1 to 2 minutes per side. Transfer to the paper towel–lined plate, and repeat one more time with the remaining oil and tofu. Transfer the crispy tofu to a serving bowl.

3 Arrange the lettuce, carrot, cucumber, mint, and scallions in individual piles on a platter. Cover with plastic wrap for now.

4 Bring a pot of water to a boil over high heat and cook the vermicelli until tender yet firm, about 10 seconds. Shock the noodles under cold running water to stop the cooking. Drain and set aside, covered, until ready to use.

Recipe continues on next page

CRISPY TOFU SALAD ROLLS,
continued

5 To make the peanut sauce, combine the peanut butter, coconut milk, hoisin, lemon juice, agave nectar, and Sriracha in a medium bowl.

6 To assemble the rolls, fill a round baking dish with room-temperature water. Place one rice paper in it and let it soak for about 10 seconds. Transfer the paper to a clean wooden cutting board (the wood surface absorbs excess water from the paper as it softens).

On the side closest to you and 1 inch from the edge, place a lettuce leaf, then add a small amount each of vermicelli, carrot, cucumber, and scallions and top with 1 tofu stick and 2 or 3 overlapped mint leaves. Taking the side closest to you, fold the rice paper somewhat tightly over the ingredients (be careful not to tear the paper). Fold in the sides, then keep rolling tightly to the end to form a roll.

Repeat with the remaining rice papers and ingredients. Serve the rolls with the peanut sauce for dipping.

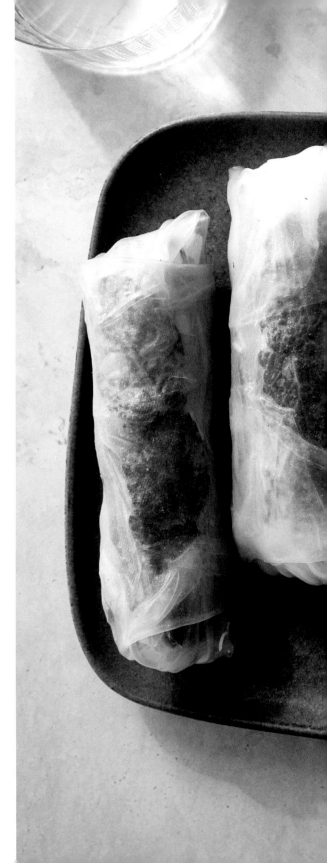

Tofu Chopped Salad
with Chipotle-Lime-Avocado Dressing

SERVES 4

All the fun of making a chopped salad is improvising based on what is in the fridge, including leftovers. A good mixture of textures, flavors, and colors is key. Think crunchy and tender, sweet and savory, red and green, and you have the makings of a beautiful combination. Consider the ingredients in this recipe as optional and inspirational. Do as you wish! As for the dressing, unlike many salad dressings, this one does not include oil. The ripe avocado is rich enough to counterbalance the lime juice.

FOR THE DRESSING

- 1 small ripe **Hass avocado**, halved, pitted, and peeled
- ½ bunch **cilantro**, stems included
- Juice of 1 **lime**
- 1 **chipotle chile** in adobo sauce
- 1 tablespoon **adobo sauce**
- 1 small **garlic clove**
- **Kosher salt** and freshly ground **black pepper**

FOR THE CHOPPED SALAD

- 1 (14-ounce) container **extra-firm regular tofu**, drained (page 7)
- 2 tablespoons **grapeseed** or **vegetable oil**
- 1 **English cucumber**, halved lengthwise, seeded, peeled (optional), and diced
- 1 **red bell pepper**, halved, stem and seeds removed, and diced
- 1 cup **edamame**, blanched
- 4 large **red radishes**, diced
- 1 sweet or tart **apple**, halved, cored, and diced
- 1 (15-ounce) can **black beans**, rinsed and drained
- 1 cup whole or lightly crushed **raw nuts** (almonds, hazelnuts, pistachios, walnuts, and so on, or a combination)
- ½ cup fresh yellow **corn kernels**
- ¼ cup **pumpkin seeds**, **sunflower seeds**, or a combination
- 2 **scallions**, root ends and tough green tops trimmed, white and green parts chopped

Recipe continues on next page

TOFU CHOPPED SALAD,
continued

1 To make the dressing, combine the avocado, cilantro, lime juice, chile, adobo sauce, and garlic in a blender, adding some water as needed to process to a smooth consistency of loose custard (that is, not too thick and not too thin). Season to taste with salt and black pepper. Set aside.

2 Cut the tofu cake in half lengthwise, then cut each half lengthwise again. Flip the 4 rectangular slices flat onto your cutting board, then cut each rectangle in half lengthwise to make 8 sticks. Cut each stick in half crosswise, then halve crosswise again to get 16 "wings." If you prefer smaller bites, cut the wings in half to make 32 nuggets (see page 8).

3 Line a plate with paper towels. Heat the oil in a large nonstick pan over medium heat. When hot, gently add the tofu and cook until crispy on all sides, 1 to 2 minutes total. Drain on the paper towel–lined plate.

4 To make the salad, toss together the cucumber, bell pepper, edamame, radishes, apple, black beans, nuts, corn, seeds, scallions, and crispy tofu in a large shallow bowl. Serve with the dressing drizzled over the salad or on the side.

TIPS | Dice the vegetables and apple approximately the same size; the smaller the cut, the more variety in each bite (I like ¼ to ½ inch). Dice the tofu larger to keep it from falling apart when panfrying.

Feel free to substitute plain unsalted roasted nuts and seeds for the raw.

Roasted Cauliflower Tofu Soup

Roasted caramelized cauliflower and garlic, fresh herbs, and a touch of fragrant curry spice result in this hearty soup. Add Crispy Soy-Sesame Tofu Nuggets for extra texture.

SERVES 4

1   head **cauliflower** (or broccoli), leaves removed, head separated into florets

3   tablespoons plus 1 teaspoon **olive oil**

1   tablespoon **curry powder**

    Kosher salt and freshly ground **black pepper**

1   large head **garlic**

2   cups **water**

1   (12-ounce) container **silken tofu**

1   tablespoon **liquid aminos** or **soy sauce**

    Freshly ground **black pepper**

    Smoked paprika, for garnish

3   **thyme sprigs**, leaves only, for garnish

3   **oregano sprigs**, leaves only, for garnish

    Crispy Soy-Sesame Tofu Nuggets (page 20; optional)

1   Preheat the oven to 400°F (200°C). Line a baking pan with parchment paper.

2   Toss the cauliflower with 3 tablespoons oil and the curry powder in a large mixing bowl. Season to taste with salt and pepper. Scatter on the baking pan. Slice off the very top of the garlic head, enough to reveal the cloves. Place the head cut side up on a piece of aluminum foil large enough to envelop it. Drizzle with the remaining 1 teaspoon oil and wrap to secure. Roast the garlic alongside the cauliflower for about 40 minutes, or until both are caramelized.

3   Scoop out the caramelized garlic and add it to a food processor along with the cauliflower, water, tofu, and liquid aminos. Process until smooth, then transfer to a medium saucepan over medium-low heat. Bring to a gentle boil and adjust the seasoning with salt and pepper.

4   Serve hot, garnishing individual servings of the soup with a sprinkling of smoked paprika and some fresh thyme and oregano leaves. Top with tofu nuggets, if desired.

Hot-and-Sour Tofu Soup

SERVES 4

A favorite on Chinese American restaurant menus, hot-and-sour soup is a classic that will please all. This version includes shiitake mushrooms, bamboo shoots, and peas in a vinegar-infused broth that works its way deep into each morsel of spongy tofu. A touch of chili oil and some scallions round out the flavor.

FOR THE BROTH

- 2 tablespoons **grapeseed** or **vegetable oil**
- 1 (2-inch) piece fresh **ginger**, thinly sliced lengthwise
- 3 large **garlic cloves**, crushed
- 3 **scallions**, root ends and tough green tops trimmed, white and green parts knotted
- 2 **carrots**, peeled and cut into large chunks
- 1 small **daikon** or 1 large round **radish**, cut into large chunks
- ¼ small head **green cabbage**, shredded
- 12 dried **shiitake mushrooms**, rinsed
- 3 quarts **water**

FOR THE SOUP

- 1 (14-ounce) container **soft regular tofu**, drained (page 7)
- ⅓ cup **rice vinegar**
- 2 tablespoons **soy sauce**
- 1 tablespoon **liquid aminos** or **soy sauce** (optional)
- 2 teaspoons **toasted sesame oil**
- 2 teaspoons **chili oil**

  Pinch of **sugar**

  Kosher salt and freshly ground **white pepper** or **black pepper**

- 12 fresh **shiitake mushrooms**, stems removed and caps julienned
- 1 (5-ounce) can julienned **bamboo shoots**, rinsed several times and drained
- 1 cup frozen **peas**
- 2–3 tablespoons **cornstarch** mixed with ¼ cup **water**
- 1 **scallion**, root end and tough green top trimmed, white and green parts chopped, for garnish

1 To make the broth, heat the oil in a large stockpot over high heat. Add the ginger, garlic, and scallions, and stir-fry until golden, about 2 minutes. Add the carrots and daikon, and stir-fry until golden brown, about 10 minutes. Stir in the cabbage, dried shiitakes, and water. Reduce the heat to medium-low, partially cover with the lid, and gently boil until reduced by half, about 2 hours. Strain the broth into a large bowl and discard the solids.

2 Cut the tofu cake in half crosswise, then cut each half crosswise into thirds. Flip the 6 short rectangular slices flat onto your cutting board. Cut each rectangle lengthwise into thirds, making 18 long sticks. Cut each of the sticks in half crosswise, and then cut each of those in half crosswise again. You should have 72 croutons about ½ inch thick (see page 9).

3 To make the soup, transfer 1½ quarts of the broth to a medium stockpot over high heat. Add the vinegar, soy sauce, liquid aminos (if using), sesame oil, and chili oil. Bring to a boil. Reduce the heat to medium-low, add the sugar, and season to taste with salt and white pepper. Stir in the fresh shiitakes, bamboo shoots, peas, and tofu, and bring to a gentle boil. Whisk in the cornstarch slurry, continuously stirring until the soup is thickened, about 3 minutes. Serve the soup hot, garnishing individual servings with scallions.

3
Sandwiches and More

Whether you're off to work, on a hike, or relaxing at the park, the beach, or poolside and craving a delicious fuss-free lunch, these recipes will save you time on prep. Organize the ingredients ahead of time, storing each separately in the refrigerator for convenience and easy reach. For optimal freshness, be sure to assemble these handheld foods just before enjoying them.

TLT&A Sandwich

SERVES 4

Any kind of sliced bread will do for this tofu, lettuce, tomato, and avocado sandwich, but I prefer whole-grain bread. The creamy, rich avocado adds flavor and texture to this vegan version of the classic BLT.

1 (14-ounce) container **extra-firm regular tofu**, drained (page 7)

2 tablespoons **grapeseed** or **vegetable oil**

2 tablespoons **liquid aminos** or **soy sauce**

1 cup cooked **chickpeas**

2 tablespoons **tahini**

1 tablespoon fresh-squeezed **lemon juice**

2 tablespoons chopped fresh **parsley**, **cilantro**, or **chives**

Pinch of **cayenne pepper** (optional)

Kosher salt and freshly ground **black pepper**

8 slices **whole-grain bread** (toasting is optional)

4 large tender **lettuce leaves**

1 medium to large ripe **tomato**, cut into 8 slices crosswise

1 whole ripe **avocado**, halved, each half sliced lengthwise into 8 pieces

1 Cut the tofu cake crosswise into 8 equal-size rectangles.

2 Set an oven rack in the center position and preheat the broiler for 10 minutes. Line a baking pan with parchment paper.

3 Stir together the oil and liquid aminos in a small bowl. Brush the tofu pieces with the mixture and place them in a single layer on the prepared baking pan. Broil for about 2 minutes, until heated through and golden on top. Turn each piece over and broil for another 2 minutes.

4 Place the chickpeas, tahini, lemon juice, parsley, and cayenne (if using) in a food processor. Process until smooth, adding a little water if necessary. Season the hummus to taste with salt and pepper.

5 To assemble the TLT&A, spread some hummus on a slice of bread (toasted or not). Layer on 2 tofu slices (one next to the other), a lettuce leaf, 2 tomato slices, and 4 slices of avocado. Top with another slice of bread. Gently press on the sandwich and slice on the diagonal. Repeat this step to make 3 more sandwiches.

Tofu Veggie Burger

SERVES 6

Tofu is a great ingredient to add to veggie burgers. It lightens the texture and provides contrast to otherwise pasty, starchy bean or lentil patties. All sorts of vegetables and herbs can be added for texture and flavor alternatives. Serve the burgers on sliced bread, potato buns, grilled portobello mushrooms, or a bed of salad greens.

1   (14-ounce) container **extra-firm regular tofu**

¼   cup **grapeseed** or **vegetable oil**

1   small **onion**, minced

1   large **garlic clove**, minced

1   small **carrot**, peeled and shredded

1   **celery stalk**, peeled and minced

1   small **zucchini**, shredded

10   **mushrooms**, minced

¼   cup chopped fresh **parsley**

1   teaspoon fresh **thyme** leaves

   Kosher salt and freshly ground **black pepper**

2   medium **eggs**

1   tablespoon **tomato paste**

   Cornstarch or **tapioca starch**, for dusting

1   Place a triple layer of paper towels on a large plate, set the tofu cake on top, then cover with another triple layer of paper towels. Drain for 1 hour, changing the paper towels every 15 minutes or when soaked. Then transfer the tofu to a bowl and crumble with a fork or with your hands.

2   Meanwhile, heat 2 tablespoons of the oil in a large skillet over medium heat. Add the onion and garlic and cook until translucent, about 5 minutes. Stir in the carrot and celery and cook until wilted and light brown, about 10 minutes. Add the zucchini, mushrooms, parsley, and thyme, and cook until light brown, about 10 minutes. Season to taste with salt and pepper, toss, and remove from the heat. Let cool, draining if necessary.

3   Whisk together the eggs and tomato paste in a large bowl until well combined. Mix in the tofu and cooled sautéed vegetables. Shape the mixture into 6 patties, dusting each all around with cornstarch.

4   Heat the remaining 2 tablespoons oil in a large nonstick pan over medium heat. Add the veggie burgers and pan-crisp until browned on both sides, about 5 minutes total.

Vietnamese Tofu Banh Mi

SERVES 6

This is a vegan version of the very popular Vietnamese pork-based sandwich. *Note:* You'll have more pickled vegetables than you'll need. Refrigerate them and enjoy the leftovers as a side with any grilled protein over rice—a typical combination in many parts of Asia.

FOR THE PICKLED VEGETABLES

- 1 quart **rice vinegar**
- ⅓ cup **sugar**
- 3 tablespoons **kosher salt**
- 2 large **carrots**, peeled and cut into 2-inch-long matchsticks
- 1 small to medium **English cucumber**, halved, cored, and cut into ¼- by 2-inch matchsticks
- 1 small **daikon**, peeled and cut into 2-inch-long matchsticks

FOR THE SANDWICHES

- 2 (14-ounce) containers **extra-firm regular tofu**, drained (page 7)
- 1 large **garlic clove**, finely grated
- 1 small **lemongrass stalk**, finely grated (see Tip)
- 1½ tablespoons **fish sauce**
- 2 teaspoons **agave nectar**
- ¼ cup **grapeseed** or **vegetable oil**
- 2 **baguettes**, each cut diagonally into 3 equal pieces
- 12 medium **oak leaf lettuce leaves**
  Sambal oelek or **Sriracha sauce** (optional)
- 12 **cilantro sprigs**, tough stems removed

TIP | Lemongrass is a tough fibrous grass, so shave it with a Microplane grater to break it down to a fine, moist powder.

1 To make the pickles, whisk together the vinegar, sugar, and salt in a large bowl until the granules are completely dissolved.

2 Place the carrots, cucumber, and daikon into their own individual 1-gallon resealable bags. Pour an equal amount of pickling liquid into each bag, then seal and squeeze out the air. Let sit for at least 1 hour. Drain out the liquid, gently squeezing each vegetable to remove excess moisture, then place the vegetables in individual bowls.

3 Cut each tofu cake in half crosswise, then cut each half crosswise into 3 equally thick rectangles. You should have a total of 12 rectangles about ½ inch thick (see page 10). While the vegetables macerate, stir together the garlic, lemongrass, fish sauce, and agave nectar in a baking dish. Add the tofu in a single layer, making sure to coat each slice. Let sit for 20 minutes.

4 Line a plate with paper towels. Heat the oil in a nonstick skillet over medium-high heat. Add the tofu and panfry until crispy, about 2 minutes per side. Transfer to the paper towel–lined plate.

5 To assemble the sandwiches, slice open each piece of baguette lengthwise. Remove some of the white crumb, if desired. Line the inside of each piece with 1 or 2 lettuce leaves (depending on their size). Add some pickled daikon, carrot, and cucumber, followed by a slice of tofu. Top with some sambal oelek, if using, and garnish with 2 cilantro sprigs.

Tofu Burritos

SERVES 4

Shredded and chopped raw and cooked ingredients, with rice, guacamole, and salsa—a medley of textures, with crumbled tofu replacing the meat protein—makes this version of the classic Mexican or Tex-Mex burrito a wholesome and delicious vegetarian option. Substitute nutritional yeast for the cheese for a vegan option.

FOR THE GUACAMOLE

- 2 ripe **Hass avocados**, halved, pitted, and crushed
- Juice of 1 **lime**
- 8 **cilantro sprigs**, leaves only
- ½ small **shallot**, minced
- **Kosher salt** and freshly ground **black pepper**

FOR THE RED SALSA

- 1 large ripe **beefsteak tomato**, peeled, seeded, and finely chopped (see Tips)
- 1 **jalapeño**, charred over a flame or under a broiler, then peeled, stem and seeds removed, and minced
- 1 **scallion**, root end and tough green top trimmed, white and green parts finely sliced
- 1 medium **garlic clove**, minced
- Juice of 1 **lime**
- **Kosher salt** and freshly ground **black pepper**

FOR THE BURRITOS

- 2 tablespoons **grapeseed** or **vegetable oil**
- ½ small **shallot**, minced
- 1 (14-ounce) container **firm regular tofu**, drained (page 7) and crumbled
- 1 teaspoon **chili powder**
- ½ teaspoon **cumin powder**
- 2 **thyme sprigs**
- **Kosher salt** and freshly ground **black pepper**
- 4 large **tortillas**, plain, whole wheat, whole grain, or flavored, warmed (see Tips)
- 1½ cups cooked **white** or **brown long-grain rice**, hot
- 1 cup grated **Jack cheese** or ⅓ cup **nutritional yeast**

1 To make the guacamole, mash the avocado with the lime juice, cilantro, and shallot in a medium bowl. Season lightly with salt and pepper. Set aside.

2 To make the red salsa, mix together the tomato, jalapeño, scallion, garlic, and lime juice in another medium bowl. Season lightly with salt and pepper. Set aside.

3 To make the burritos, heat the oil in a medium nonstick pan over medium heat. Add the shallot and sauté until golden, about 3 minutes. Stir in the tofu, chili powder, cumin, and thyme. Season lightly with salt and pepper. Divide into 4 portions.

4 To assemble the burritos, lay out a softened tortilla and scatter one-quarter of the rice on the lower third. Top the rice with a portion of tofu and then some cheese, guacamole, and salsa, in that order, spreading the ingredients evenly. Taking the side closest to you, fold the tortilla over the filling tightly, fold in the sides, and keep rolling to the end. Repeat this step with the remaining tortillas and ingredients.

5 If desired, place each burrito in a dry or lightly oiled grill pan over medium heat. Press the top with a spatula until crispy and lightly charred on one side, 1 to 2 minutes. Flip over carefully and repeat on the other side.

TIPS | To peel the tomato, bring a small pot of water to a boil over high heat. Using a knife, score the tomato on one end with a crisscross pattern. Dip in the hot water for 15 seconds. Drain, let cool, and peel. Quarter the tomato and remove the seeds.

Before using the tortillas, warm them in a dry pan over medium heat for a few seconds to soften (not crisp).

Grilled Tofu Pita Pocket
with Mint Tahini

SERVES 4

On its own, tahini (sesame paste) can be bitter. Adding lemon juice, refreshing mint, and naturally sweet roasted garlic results in a balanced flavor. Choose crunchy salad greens to complement the tender tofu.

1	small head **garlic**
1	teaspoon **olive oil**
⅓	cup **tahini**
3	tablespoons fresh-squeezed **lemon juice**
6	large **mint leaves**
	Pinch of **cayenne pepper**
2	tablespoons **water** (optional)
	Kosher salt
1	(14-ounce) container **extra-firm regular tofu**, drained (page 7)
3	tablespoons **grapeseed** or **vegetable oil**
4	**pita pockets**, warmed, sliced around ⅓ of the edge to open
4–6	**romaine lettuce leaves**, julienned
1	**Persian cucumber**, diced
1	ripe medium **tomato**, stem and seeds removed, diced
	Paprika, for garnish
1	tablespoon chopped **chives**, for garnish

1 Preheat the oven to 400°F (200°C).

2 Slice off the very top of the garlic head, just enough to reveal the cloves. Place the head cut side up on a piece of aluminum foil large enough to envelop it. Drizzle with the olive oil and wrap to secure. Place on a baking pan and roast for about 40 minutes, or until tender, golden, and fragrant.

3 With a butter knife, remove the roasted cloves from the skin and transfer to a blender or food processor. Add the tahini, lemon juice, mint, and cayenne. Process, adding the water as needed to reach the desired consistency. (The sauce should be like loose custard—that is, not too thick and not too thin.) Season to taste with salt.

4 Cut the tofu cake crosswise into 8 equal slices. Heat the grapeseed oil in a large nonstick grill pan over medium-high heat. Grill the tofu squares until browned on both sides, about 5 minutes total. (Wait until the tofu is browned before flipping, or the crispy part will stick to the pan rather than lift effortlessly.)

5 To assemble, gently pry open a warm pita. Insert some lettuce, cucumber, and tomato, then 2 slices of tofu, then more vegetables. Drizzle with tahini sauce, sprinkle with paprika, and garnish with chives.

Tofu Quesadilla

SERVES 4

Roasted sweet bell peppers and onions are some of the most basic and flavorful ingredients available. Use different-colored bell peppers in this recipe for visual appeal. Other combinations that work well are spinach with mushrooms and corn with sautéed cherry tomatoes.

1   medium **red onion**, cut into ¼-inch slices, rings separated

1   **red bell pepper**, halved, stem and seeds removed, cut into ¼-inch strips

1   **orange bell pepper**, halved, stem and seeds removed, cut into ¼-inch strips

1   **yellow bell pepper**, halved, stem and seeds removed, cut into ¼-inch strips

1   **green bell pepper**, halved, stem and seeds removed, cut into ¼-inch strips

2   tablespoons **olive oil**

Kosher salt and freshly ground **black pepper**

1   (14-ounce) container **soft regular tofu**, drained (page 7)

8   medium **tortillas**, plain, whole wheat, whole grain, or flavored, warmed

1   cup grated **Jack cheese**

⅓   cup **pickled jalapeño**, drained

1   Preheat the oven to 400°F (200°C).

2   Toss together the onion and red, orange, yellow, and green bell peppers in a large mixing bowl. Add the oil, stir, and season to taste with salt and black pepper. Scatter onto two baking pans and roast for about 40 minutes, or until charred, tossing after 15 and 25 minutes.

3   Cut the tofu cake in half crosswise, then cut each half crosswise into 3 equally thick rectangles for a total of 6 rectangles. Flip each rectangle flat onto your cutting board. Cut each in half crosswise for a total of 12 squares about ½ inch thick (see page 11).

4   To assemble, lay out a tortilla and scatter on some cheese. Top with 3 slices of tofu. Scatter on another layer of cheese and top with some roasted vegetables and jalapeño. Sprinkle lightly with more cheese and top with another tortilla. Repeat this step with the remaining tortillas to make 4 quesadillas.

5   Heat a large skillet over medium heat. Place a quesadilla in the skillet and cook until the cheese is melted and the tortilla is crisp, 1 to 2 minutes. Flip and crisp the other side, 1 to 2 minutes longer. Repeat with the remaining quesadillas. Alternatively, divide the quesadillas between two baking pans and bake in a preheated 400°F (200°C) oven for 10 to 15 minutes, or until the cheese is melted and the tortilla is crisp.

Baked Tofu and Spinach Empanadas

MAKES 8 EMPANADAS

These oven-crisp empanadas are light and filling in the same bite. Easy to grab, they make a perfect snack or meal on the go. In this recipe, weighting the tofu to help it drain will prevent the filling from becoming too wet and ensure a crispy rather than soggy crust. You can serve empanadas with red or green salsa on the side.

1 (14-ounce) container **firm regular tofu**, drained (page 7)

1¼ cups **all-purpose flour**, plus more for dusting

¼ cup **whole-wheat flour**

½ teaspoon **kosher salt**

6 tablespoons **butter**, chilled and cut into ½-inch dice

2 **eggs**

¼ cup plus 1–2 tablespoons chilled **water**

3 tablespoons **olive oil**

1 medium **onion**, minced

2 large **garlic cloves**, minced

8 tightly packed cups previously frozen **spinach**, water squeezed out

1 teaspoon **smoked paprika**

½ teaspoon **ground nutmeg**

2 teaspoons **cornstarch** or **tapioca starch**

Kosher salt and freshly ground **black pepper**

1 Place a triple layer of paper towels on a large plate, set the tofu cake on top, then cover with another triple layer of paper towels. Weight the tofu for 30 minutes to 1 hour to press out excess water, changing the paper towels when drenched.

2 Sift together the all-purpose flour, whole-wheat flour, and salt in a large mixing bowl. With your fingertips, work in the butter until the mixture has a coarse meal consistency. Make a well in the center. Add 1 of the eggs and 2 tablespoons of the water. Using a fork, stir to combine the ingredients. Add another tablespoon or two of chilled water if the dough is too dry to come together.

3 Dust your work surface with all-purpose flour. Turn out the dough and knead until it holds together well. (Do not overwork the dough, or it will get tough when baked.) Shape into a thick disk, wrap in plastic wrap, and refrigerate for 30 minutes or until ready to use.

Recipe continues on next page

BAKED TOFU AND SPINACH EMPANADAS,
continued

4 Heat the oil in a large skillet over medium heat. Add the onion and garlic and sauté until light brown, about 10 minutes. Add the spinach, paprika, and nutmeg. Toss well and cook until heated through, about 15 minutes.

Crumble the tofu and toss into the vegetable mixture along with the cornstarch, season to taste with salt and pepper, and remove from the heat to cool. Divide this filling into 8 equal portions.

5 Divide the dough into 8 equal pieces and form them into balls. Cover them loosely with plastic wrap to keep them from drying out.

6 Whisk together the remaining egg with 2 tablespoons water in a small bowl. Set this egg wash aside.

7 Set an oven rack in the center position and preheat the oven to 400°F (200°C). Line a baking pan with parchment paper.

8 Working with one dough ball at a time, flatten it into a disk and roll it out thin, to about 8 inches in diameter. Add one portion of the filling to the center of the disk, leaving about a ¾-inch edge, void of filling, all around. Fold the dough over the filling to create a half-moon. Roll and twist the edge to secure the filling. Brush the top of the empanada with egg wash. Repeat with the remaining dough balls and filling.

9 Place the empanadas on the prepared baking pan and bake for 15 to 20 minutes, until golden.

4

Family Favorites

On a cool night, we warm up by turning on the oven or cooking low and slow by braising or stewing. In this chapter you'll find some of the most classic and popular family foods, the kind you grew up eating in multiple variations—recipes passed down from generation to generation or enjoyed at your favorite neighborhood restaurant. Bolognese, lasagna, quiche—whatever it is, each of the recipes here has a delicious, wholesome tofu twist for guilt-free eating.

Tofu-Cucumber Raita over Baked Potatoes

SERVES 4 (MAKES ABOUT 2 CUPS)

Yogurt sauce is a popular condiment in Indian cuisine, where it is known as raita. Inspired by the dairy-based classic, this tofu version is refreshing with cucumber, cilantro, and lemon, helping to keep the palate cool and taming all sorts of spicy foods. It's also delicious scooped over flaky baked potatoes.

1   medium **English cucumber**, peeled, halved, seeded, and grated

1   (12-ounce) container **silken tofu**

Juice of 1 **lemon**

½   teaspoon **cumin powder**

8   large **mint leaves**, minced

4   **cilantro sprigs**, leaves only, minced

1   small to medium **garlic clove**, finely grated

Kosher salt

4   medium to large baked **russet potatoes**, hot

4   **chives**, chopped, for garnish

1   Grab a handful of grated cucumber and squeeze out the natural water. Transfer the pulp to a bowl. Repeat with the remaining cucumber.

2   Whisk together the tofu, lemon juice, and cumin in a medium bowl. Stir in the cucumber, mint, cilantro, and garlic. Season to taste with salt.

3   Split open the potatoes lengthwise. Use a fork to fluff the pulp, then top with some tofu raita and garnish with chives.

Baked Tofu Loaf

SERVES 8

Meatless Monday calls for a baked tofu loaf, infused with fragrant dried shiitakes. Eggs are used as a binder, but feel free to use a vegan option. Peas and carrots provide color and natural sweetness to the loaf. I love a good sweet-and-sour Asian-inspired sauce for glazing; feel free to adjust the sweetness level to your liking.

FOR THE LOAF

- 3 tablespoons **grapeseed** or **vegetable oil**, plus more for greasing
- 1 medium **onion**, minced
- 1 large **garlic clove**, minced
- 1 (2-inch) piece fresh **ginger**, peeled and minced
- 8 dried **shiitake mushrooms**, soaked in water until soft, stems removed, and caps chopped (see Tip)
- 1 large **celery stalk**, peeled and finely diced
- 1 medium **carrot**, peeled and finely diced
- 1 small bunch **cilantro**, stems trimmed lightly, coarsely chopped
- 2 (14-ounce) containers **extra-firm regular tofu**, drained (page 7) and crumbled
- 2 **eggs**, whisked
- 2 tablespoons **soy sauce**
- 1 tablespoon **toasted sesame oil**

FOR THE GLAZE

- 1 tablespoon **grapeseed** or **vegetable oil**
- 1 (2-inch) piece fresh **ginger**, peeled and finely grated
- 1 **scallion**, root end and tough green top trimmed, white and green parts minced
- ⅓ cup **soy sauce**
- ¼ cup **water**
- Juice of 1 **lemon**
- 2–3 teaspoons **Sriracha sauce**
- 1–2 tablespoons **sugar**
- 2 teaspoons **cornstarch** mixed with 1 tablespoon **water**

1 Preheat the oven to 375°F (190°C). Thoroughly grease a nonstick 9-inch loaf pan.

2 To make the loaf, heat the grapeseed oil in a large skillet over medium heat. Add the onion and garlic and sauté until light brown, about 10 minutes. Add the ginger and mushrooms and cook until tender, about 7 minutes. Add the celery and carrot and cook until softened, about 5 minutes. Stir in the cilantro and remove from the heat to cool completely.

3 Mix the cooled vegetables, tofu, eggs, soy sauce, and sesame oil in a large bowl. Transfer the mixture to the prepared loaf pan, making sure to spread and press it down evenly throughout. Cover with aluminum foil and bake for 35 minutes. Leave the oven on.

4 To make the glaze, heat the grapeseed oil in a small saucepan over medium heat. Add the ginger and scallion and sauté until fragrant, about 1 minute. Reduce the heat to low and whisk in the soy sauce, water, lemon juice, Sriracha, and sugar. Bring to a gentle boil. Add the cornstarch slurry and cook, continuously whisking, until the sauce thickens, about 1 minute.

5 Brush half the glaze over the tofu loaf and bake, uncovered, for 10 to 15 minutes. Remove from the oven, brush on the remaining glaze, and place the pan on a wire rack to cool for 15 to 20 minutes. Cut into ¾-inch-thick slices to serve.

TIP | I prefer dried shiitake mushrooms because they have a concentrated perfume and are a different variety than the very mild readily available types, but you can use fresh shiitakes here as well. Alternatively, you can substitute fresh white or baby bella mushrooms; just add a few more for a more pronounced flavor.

Zucchini-Spinach-Tofu "Ricotta" Lasagna

SERVES 8

Lasagna is an easy-to-make one-dish meal. Layered with roasted zucchini, spinach, and naturally sweet and tangy tomato sauce, this version is balanced with tofu "ricotta," a rich and complete protein. Serve alongside a salad. For a vegan version, skip the mozzarella and use ⅓ cup nutritional yeast instead of the egg. It acts as a binder and has a cheesy flavor.

⅓ cup **olive oil**

1 small **onion**, chopped

3 large **garlic cloves**, minced

1 (28-ounce) can San Marzano peeled **tomatoes**, crushed

Kosher salt and freshly ground **black pepper**

4 **basil sprigs**, leaves only

12 pieces **lasagna pasta** (strips or sheets, dried or fresh)

2 (14-ounce) containers **firm** or **extra-firm regular tofu**, drained (page 7) and crumbled

1 extra-large **egg**, whisked

4 **oregano sprigs**, leaves only

6–8 medium **zucchini** or **yellow squash**, sliced into ¹⁄₁₆-inch-thick rounds (see Tip, page 80)

2 (1-pound) bags frozen **spinach**, thawed and drained

1 pound **mozzarella cheese**, thinly sliced

1 Heat the oil in a saucepan over medium heat. Add the onion and garlic and sauté until golden, about 10 minutes. Reduce the heat to low, add the tomatoes, and cook until reduced by one-quarter, about 25 minutes. Season to taste with salt and pepper, then stir in the basil and remove the pan from the heat.

2 Preheat the oven to 375°F (190°C).

3 Bring a large pot of salted water to a boil and cook the pasta according to the package directions. Shock the pasta under cold running water to stop the cooking, drain, and lay it flat.

4 Meanwhile, combine the tofu, egg, and oregano in a medium bowl. Season lightly with salt and pepper.

Recipe continues on next page

ZUCCHINI-SPINACH-TOFU "RICOTTA" LASAGNA,
continued

5 Spread one ladle of tomato sauce over the bottom of a glass 9- by 13-inch baking dish. Add one layer of pasta (4 strips, slightly over-lapped), then spread half of the tofu "ricotta" on top. Add half the zucchini, slightly overlapping and arranging the rounds in long rows following the length or the width (pick one for consistency) of the pasta sheets. Then scatter half the spinach over the zucchini slices. Add another layer of pasta, then sauce, then tofu, zucchini, and spin-ach. Finish with a final layer of pasta topped with sauce, followed by the mozzarella.

6 Cover the dish loosely with aluminum foil and bake for about 35 minutes, until bubbly. Uncover and bake for 10 minutes longer, until golden. Let cool for 15 minutes before slicing.

TIP Choose zucchini or yellow squash that is firm to the touch and no bigger than medium in size. Large ones tend to have a softer seedy core, which renders a watery texture when cooked.

Tofu "Paneer" in Spicy Creamed Spinach

SERVES 4

Paneer is a mild-tasting firm white cheese used in Indian cooking. It is often pan-crisped and added to a spinach-based dish called saag paneer. Tofu is a perfect substitute, resembling paneer in texture and color. It also happens to be mild in flavor. Serve this dish with basmati rice or a flatbread, such as naan, on the side.

1 (14-ounce) container **extra-firm regular tofu**, drained (page 7)

¼ cup **coconut oil**

1 small **onion**, finely chopped

1 large **garlic clove**, minced

1 (1-inch) piece fresh **ginger**, peeled and minced

1 **jalapeño**, halved, stem and seeds removed, and minced (see Tip)

2 teaspoons **garam masala**

1 teaspoon **cumin powder**

1 teaspoon **ground coriander**

1½ pounds frozen **spinach**, thawed

8 **cilantro sprigs**, trimmed and finely chopped

1 cup unsweetened **coconut milk**

2–3 tablespoons fresh-squeezed **lemon juice**

Kosher salt and freshly ground **black pepper**

Pinch of **cayenne pepper** (optional)

1 Cut the tofu cake in half lengthwise, then cut each half lengthwise again. Flip the 4 rectangular slices flat onto your cutting board, then cut each rectangle in half lengthwise to make 8 sticks. Cut each stick in half crosswise, then halve crosswise again. You should have 32 nuggets (see page 8).

2 Heat 2 tablespoons of the oil in a medium to large pan over medium heat. Add the onion, garlic, and ginger, and sauté until golden, about 5 minutes. Add the jalapeño, garam masala, cumin, and coriander, and stir until fragrant, about 30 seconds. Reduce the heat to low and stir in the spinach, cilantro, coconut milk, and lemon juice. Season to taste with salt and black pepper. Cook down, stirring occasionally, to a chunky purée consistency, about 20 minutes. Stir in the cayenne, if desired.

3 Meanwhile, heat the remaining 2 tablespoons oil in a nonstick skillet over medium-high heat. Add the tofu cubes and cook until golden and crispy on all sides, about 1 minute per side. Be sure to keep the pieces separated to prevent them from sticking together.

4 Add the crispy tofu to the creamed spinach and serve.

TIP | Not all jalapeños are created equal—some are spicier than others. Adjust the dish's spice level with cayenne pepper, if desired.

Tofu Mushroom Bolognese

SERVES 6

Everyone likes pasta. It's a quick and easy meal to throw together at the last minute. This tofu and mushroom Bolognese sauce is both deliciously rich and healthy. I love herbs and tend to use them like vegetables. Don't shy away from basil: Add a generous amount to the sauce for extra goodness.

⅓ cup **olive oil**

1 small **onion**, minced

3 large **garlic cloves**, minced

1 pound baby bella **mushrooms**, minced

1 (28-ounce) can crushed **tomatoes**

1 (14-ounce) container **firm regular tofu**, drained (page 7) and crumbled

Kosher salt and freshly ground **black pepper**

6–8 **basil sprigs**, leaves only

1 pound **spaghettini** or any pasta of choice

Grated Parmesan cheese, for garnish

Red pepper flakes, for garnish (optional)

1 Heat the oil in a large skillet over medium heat. Add the onion and garlic and cook until the onion is translucent to lightly golden, 10 to 15 minutes. Stir in the mushrooms and cook until softened, about 5 minutes. Stir in the tomatoes and cook until reduced by about one-third, about 20 minutes.

2 Add the tofu, season to taste with salt and pepper, stir to combine, and cook for 5 to 10 minutes. Reduce the heat to a gentle simmer, add half the basil leaves, and cover.

3 Meanwhile, bring a pot of salted water to a boil over high heat. Add the pasta and cook until al dente, according to the package directions. Drain.

4 Increase the heat under the sauce to medium and add the pasta, tossing it well. Serve the Bolognese on individual pasta plates, garnished with the remaining basil, Parmesan to taste, and pepper flakes, if desired.

Tex-Mex Tofu Chili

SERVES 8

Chili is comfort food, and this vegan version is, too. Wholesome, with tofu, red kidney beans, string beans, and carrots, and loaded with fresh herbs for a deep and refreshing flavor, this chili is so satisfying that carnivores won't miss the meat. As is the case for any stew—rested overnight, flavors deepened, and reheated—leftovers are even more delicious.

1	(14-ounce) container **firm regular tofu**, drained (page 7)
¼	cup **olive oil**
1	large **onion**, cut into ½-inch dice
4	large **garlic cloves**, minced
1	large **carrot**, peeled and cut into ¼-inch dice
2	**celery stalks**, peeled and cut into ¼-inch dice
2	**green bell peppers**, halved, seeded, and cut into ¼-inch dice
1	teaspoon **cumin powder**
2–3	tablespoons **chili powder**
	Cayenne pepper (optional)
1	quart low-sodium or salt-free **vegetable stock**
1	(28-ounce) can crushed **tomatoes**
8	**parsley sprigs**, leaves only, coarsely chopped
1	(14-ounce) can **red kidney beans**, rinsed several times and drained
	Kosher salt and freshly ground **black pepper**

1. Cut the tofu cake in half crosswise, then cut each half crosswise into thirds. Flip the 6 short rectangular slices flat onto your cutting board. Cut each rectangle lengthwise into thirds, making 18 long sticks. Cut each of the sticks in half crosswise, and then cut each of those in half crosswise again. You should have 72 croutons about ½ inch thick (see page 9).

2. Heat the oil in a large stockpot over medium heat. Add the onion and garlic and sauté, stirring occasionally, until golden brown, about 15 minutes. Stir in the carrot, celery, and bell peppers, and sauté until softened, about 15 minutes longer.

3. Stir in the cumin, chili powder, and cayenne to taste (if desired). Add the stock, crushed tomatoes, and parsley, and cook for 30 minutes.

4. Add the kidney beans and tofu and cook for another 30 minutes, allowing the flavors to meld together and the whole mixture to thicken slightly. Season to taste with salt and black pepper.

TIP | The consistency of chili varies from recipe to recipe. If it's too thick, add some water. If it's too thin, cook it longer, until it reaches the desired consistency. Though this dish is vegan, you can always sprinkle servings with nutritional yeast for a cheesy flavor.

Mapo Tofu

SERVES 6

Mapo tofu graces the menus of many Chinese restaurants. Though the dish is classically made by adding ground pork or beef, this vegan version is so delicious you won't miss the meat. Serve its saucy goodness over noodles or a steaming bowl of long-grain jasmine rice.

Szechuan peppercorns and Chinese chili bean sauce are unique products. Look for them at an Asian market. If you can't find them, you can omit them. The dish will still be delicious.

¼ cup **grapeseed** or **vegetable oil**

2 teaspoons **Szechuan peppercorns**, crushed

2 large **garlic cloves**, minced

1 (1½-inch) piece fresh **ginger**, peeled and grated

6 dried **shiitake mushrooms**, soaked in water until soft, stems removed, caps minced, and 1 cup of the soaking water reserved and filtered (see Tip)

2 (14-ounce) containers **soft regular tofu**, drained (page 7)

2 tablespoons **Chinese chili bean sauce**

3 dried whole **red chiles**

2 teaspoons **cornstarch** mixed with 1 tablespoon **water**

Pinch of **sugar**

½ cup fresh or frozen **peas**

2 teaspoons **toasted sesame oil**, for serving

2 **scallions**, root ends and tough green tops trimmed, white and green parts cut into ½-inch-long pieces, for garnish

1 Heat the grapeseed oil in a wok or skillet over medium-low heat. Add the peppercorns and toast until fragrant, about 15 seconds. Add the garlic and ginger and stir-fry until lightly browned, about 2 minutes. Add the mushrooms to the wok and cook until lightly browned, about 5 minutes.

2 Meanwhile, cut the tofu into roughly 1-inch cubes.

3 Add the filtered mushroom water to the wok, along with the chili bean sauce and chiles. Then add the cornstarch slurry and sugar, stirring continuously until they are fully incorporated. Once the sauce is slightly thickened, add the tofu, stirring gently so as not to break it up too much. Stir in the peas and let cook for 10 minutes. Serve hot, drizzled with sesame oil and garnished with the scallions.

TIP | To filter the mushroom soaking water, line a fine-mesh sieve with a coffee filter or paper towel, place the sieve over a bowl, and pour in the soaking water.

Tofu Vegetable Curry

SERVES 4

The word *curry* (or *kare* in Japanese) means "stew." The word also describes a spice mix or a paste, depending on where the curry comes from. Both Indian dry powder curry and Thai curry paste are readily available. Feel free to use either in this recipe. The powder will give you a mild yellow curry, while the red paste will give you a spicy, herbal, reddish version; each has its own distinct taste. Combined with coconut milk and other vegetables and served over rice or noodles, this tofu vegetable curry is delicious and filling.

1 (14-ounce) container **firm** or **extra-firm regular tofu**, drained (page 7)

3 tablespoons **grapeseed** or **vegetable oil**

1 small **onion**, chopped

1 (2-inch) piece fresh **ginger**, peeled and grated

1 large **garlic clove**, minced

10 dried **shiitake mushrooms**, soaked in water until soft, stems removed and caps quartered

1 tablespoon **Indian curry powder** or 1½ tablespoons **Thai red curry paste**

1 large ripe **tomato**, halved crosswise, seeded, and finely chopped, or 1 cup crushed **tomatoes**

1 (13.5-ounce) can **coconut milk**, stirred

1½ cups **water**

½ cup fresh or frozen **peas**

Kosher salt and freshly ground **black pepper**

½ cup **cilantro leaves**

1 Cut the tofu cake in half lengthwise, then cut each half lengthwise again. Flip the 4 rectangular slices flat onto your cutting board, then cut each rectangle in half lengthwise to make 8 sticks. Cut each stick in half crosswise, then halve crosswise again to get 16 "wings." If you prefer smaller bites, cut the wings in half to make 32 nuggets (see page 8).

2 Heat the oil in a skillet over medium heat. Add the onion, ginger, and garlic, and cook until fragrant and golden, about 10 minutes. Stir in the mushrooms and curry powder and cook until the vegetables are softened, about 10 minutes. Add the tomato and cook for 10 to 15 minutes more.

3 Add the coconut milk and water. Cook, stirring occasionally, until reduced and thickened, about 30 minutes.

4 Stir in the tofu and peas, then season to taste with salt and pepper. Cook until all the ingredients are hot, about 10 minutes longer. Add the cilantro and serve.

Kimchi Tofu Stew

SERVES 4

Kimchi, a popular Korean condiment, is readily available and excellent added to many types of recipes, including jjigae, a traditional stew with many variations. You can make this tofu version more or less saucy by adjusting the cooking time, depending on your desired consistency. It's warming and perfect on a cold day.

1 (14-ounce) container **soft**, **firm**, or **extra-firm regular tofu**, drained (page 7)

¼ cup **grapeseed** or **vegetable oil**

1 small **onion**, halved and sliced into thin wedges

1 (2-inch) piece fresh **ginger**, peeled and finely julienned

1 large **garlic clove**, minced

8 dried **shiitake mushrooms**, soaked in water until soft, stems removed, caps julienned, and 2 cups of the soaking water reserved and filtered (see Tip, page 85)

1⅓ cups tightly packed chopped **kimchi**

2 tablespoons **liquid aminos** or **soy sauce**

1 (2- by 3-inch) piece **kelp** (optional)

3 **scallions**, root ends and tough green tops trimmed, white and green parts cut into 1-inch pieces

1. Cut the tofu cake in half lengthwise, then cut each half lengthwise again. Flip the 4 rectangular slices flat onto your cutting board, then cut each rectangle in half lengthwise to make 8 sticks. Cut each stick in half crosswise, then halve crosswise again. You should have 32 nuggets (see page 8).

2. Heat 3 tablespoons of the oil in a medium pot over medium heat. Add the onion, ginger, and garlic, and stir-fry until golden, about 10 minutes. Add the mushrooms and stir-fry until brown, about 5 minutes. Reduce the heat to medium-low and add the mushroom soaking water, kimchi, liquid aminos, and kelp (if using). Partially cover the pot and gently boil the stew until the liquids have reduced by half, about 20 minutes.

3. Meanwhile, heat the remaining 1 tablespoon oil in a nonstick pan over medium heat. Panfry the tofu cubes until golden on all sides, about 1 minute per side. Add to the stew, along with the scallions, stir, and serve.

Potato-Crusted Tofu and Broccoli Quiche

SERVES 6

Waxy potatoes, such as red potatoes, are the perfect ingredient for making a gluten-free savory tart crust. This crispy crust is relatively light yet substantial with a tofu and broccoli filling. This recipe can easily be made with spinach, roasted bell peppers, or your favorite quiche ingredient.

4	tablespoons plus 1 teaspoon **grapeseed** or **vegetable oil**, plus more for greasing
1	large head **garlic**
1	**thyme sprig**, leaves only
2	large **waxy potatoes**, peeled and finely grated
	Kosher salt
1	medium **onion**, chopped
1	small head **broccoli**, separated into small florets, stem cut into ½-inch dice
6	**eggs**, whisked
1	(14-ounce) container **firm regular tofu**, drained (page 7) and crumbled
1	cup shredded **cheddar cheese**
⅓	cup **milk**
	Freshly ground **black pepper**

1 Set an oven rack in the center position and preheat the oven to 450°F (230°C). Thoroughly grease a nonstick 9-inch pie dish.

2 Slice off the very top of the garlic head, just enough to reveal the cloves. Place the head cut side up on a piece of aluminum foil large enough to envelop it. Drizzle with 1 teaspoon of the oil, sprinkle on the thyme, and wrap to secure. Place on a baking pan and bake for about 40 minutes, or until soft and golden. (The garlic finishes cooking while the crust bakes.)

3 Meanwhile, place the grated potatoes in a clean kitchen towel, then twist to squeeze out the natural juices. Transfer to a bowl and toss with 2 tablespoons of the oil and ½ teaspoon salt. Press the grated potatoes evenly over the bottom and sides of the prepared pie dish.

4 Place the crust on the baking pan, next to the garlic, and bake for about 25 minutes, or until golden and crisp. Set both the garlic and the crust aside to cool. Reduce the oven temperature to 375°F (190°C).

5 Meanwhile, heat the remaining 2 table- spoons oil in a medium pan over high heat. Add the onion and sauté until golden, about 10 minutes. Set aside.

6 Bring a medium pot of salted water to a boil over high heat. Blanch the broccoli until just tender, about 1 minute. Shock with cold water to stop the cooking and drain thoroughly.

7 When the garlic is cool enough to handle, remove the cloves from their sheaths, keep- ing them as intact as possible, and transfer to a large bowl. Add the onion, broccoli, eggs, tofu, cheese, and milk. Season to taste with salt and pepper and stir to distribute the ingre- dients evenly. Fill the potato crust with the mixture, and bake for about 30 minutes, or until golden and firm.

TIP | As an alternative, substitute a flour crust (see Baked Tofu and Spinach Empanadas, page 69) for the potato crust.

5

One-Dish Meals

Convenient and efficient, these one-dish meals also lessen the mess in the kitchen. Typically, one-dish meals incorporate complex carbohydrates or starches, such as rice or noodles, and include complete proteins such as beans and tofu—examples of a clean canvas upon which all sorts of ingredients can be served. Colors, textures, and flavors abound, while the juices trickle through the starchy base. These dishes can be made ahead of time and easily reheated in the microwave or over low, gentle heat.

Tofu Poke
with Sesame-Soy Dressing

SERVES 4

This simple dish allows the ingredients to shine in their most natural form. The Hawaiian poke bowl has become popular over the last few years, with shops popping up here, there, and everywhere. Fortunately, it's relatively easy to make poke at home; all you need is a good sauce and good rice.

The toppings can include a variety of colorful raw, steamed, or lightly blanched vegetables. Spice up the sauce according to your taste. In this version the tofu is added "naked" and unheated. Alternatively, it can be warmed by steaming, baking, broiling, grilling, sautéing, or pan-crisping.

1 (14-ounce) container **firm regular tofu**, drained (page 7)

½ cup **soy sauce**

2 tablespoons **mirin**

2 tablespoons **rice vinegar**

1 tablespoon **toasted sesame oil**

1 tablespoon **tahini** (optional)

2 teaspoons **Sriracha sauce** (optional)

1 (1-inch) piece fresh **ginger**, peeled and finely grated

1 **scallion**, root end and tough green top trimmed, white and green parts thinly sliced

4 cups cooked **sushi rice** (white or brown, or a combination), warm

1 cup shelled **edamame**

4 small **red radishes**, thinly sliced into rounds

8 **asparagus stalks**, trimmed and cut into 1-inch pieces, blanched (see Tip, page 96)

1 large **carrot**, peeled and shredded

1 large ripe **Hass avocado**, halved, pitted, peeled, and thinly sliced or cut into ½-inch chunks

Toasted sesame seeds, for garnish

Unseasoned roasted **macadamia nuts**, lightly crushed, for garnish (optional)

1 large **nori sheet**, quartered and cut into thin strips, for garnish (optional)

Recipe continues on page 96

TOFU POKE,
continued

1 Cut the tofu cake in half lengthwise, then cut each half lengthwise again. Flip the 4 rectangular slices flat onto your cutting board, then cut each rectangle in half lengthwise to make 8 sticks. Cut each stick in half crosswise, then halve crosswise again to get 16 "wings." If you prefer smaller bites, cut the wings in half to make 32 nuggets (see page 8).

2 Whisk together the soy sauce, mirin, vinegar, oil, tahini (if using), and Sriracha (if using) in a medium bowl until smooth. Stir in the ginger and scallion. Transfer half the sauce to a small bowl and set aside. Add the tofu to the remaining sauce in the bowl and use a spatula to gently fold it in.

3 In each of four bowls, add 1 cup of the warm rice, spreading it evenly across the bottom. Top with the vegetables, arranging the edamame, radishes, asparagus, carrot, and avocado in individual piles in each bowl, and place the tofu in the center. Drizzle some of the reserved sauce over each serving. Sprinkle with toasted sesame seeds and macadamia nuts, and garnish with strips of nori, if desired.

TIP | To blanch any vegetable, bring a pot of salted water to a boil, add the vegetable, and flash cook for 30 seconds to 2 minutes, depending on the vegetable and the size of the cut. For this recipe, blanch the asparagus for 30 seconds.

Tofu-Stuffed Poblanos
with Salsa

SERVES 4

Stuffed roasted peppers of any kind are perfect for one-dish meals. I like to use green poblanos, especially if I find large ones. I've sometimes made the recipe using medium yellow, red, or orange sweet bell peppers as a colorful alternative (see Tip on page 98).

FOR THE SALSA

3 large ripe **tomatoes**, stems and seeds removed, minced

1 large **garlic clove**, minced

1 small **shallot**, minced

1–2 **jalapeños**, stems and seeds removed, minced

Juice of 1 **lime**

4 **cilantro sprigs**, leaves only, chopped

Kosher salt and freshly ground **black pepper**

FOR THE STUFFED PEPPERS

8 large **poblano peppers**

3 tablespoons **olive oil**

1 large **onion**, chopped

1 large **garlic clove**, minced

2 **zucchini**, cut into ½-inch dice

1 cup fresh or frozen yellow **corn kernels**

1 (15-ounce) can **black beans**, rinsed and drained

1 (14-ounce) container **soft** or **firm regular tofu**, drained (page 7) and crumbled

2 cups cooked **long-grain rice**

1 cup fresh **cilantro**, leaves and thin stems, chopped

2 teaspoons **smoked paprika**

2 teaspoons **chili powder**

½ teaspoon **cumin powder**

½ teaspoon **cayenne pepper**

Kosher salt and freshly ground **black pepper**

2 cups grated **Jack cheese** (optional)

Recipe continues on next page

TOFU-STUFFED POBLANOS,
continued

1 To make the salsa, toss together the tomatoes, garlic, shallot, jalapeños, lime juice, and
cilantro in a medium bowl. Season to taste with
salt and black pepper, toss, and set aside to let
the ingredients macerate until ready to serve.

2 To make the peppers, char all sides of the
poblanos, whether on a stove, on a grill,
or under the broiler. Once they are blackened,
enclose the peppers in a paper bag for 15 minutes, allowing them to steam, softening the skin.
Then peel the peppers, keeping the stem intact.
Using a paring knife, cut a slit along one side of
each poblano to form a pocket. Carefully clean
out and discard the seeds. Drain each pepper
over a bowl to collect the natural juices, if any.

3 Set an oven rack in the center position and
preheat the oven to 400°F (200°C). Line a
baking pan with parchment paper.

4 Heat the oil in a large skillet over
medium heat. Add the onion and garlic and
sauté until light golden, about 10 minutes. Stir
in the zucchini, corn, and beans, and sauté until
the zucchini is wilted, about 5 minutes. Stir in the
tofu, rice, cilantro, paprika, chili, cumin, cayenne,
and any collected poblano juice. Stir and season
to taste with salt and black pepper. Remove from
the heat.

5 Place the roasted peppers cut side up on
the prepared baking pan. Divide the sautéed
vegetable mixture equally and stuff each pepper.
Sprinkle with the cheese, if desired. Bake for
15 minutes, or until hot and the cheese is melted.
Serve with the freshly made salsa on the side.

TIP │ If substituting bell peppers for the poblanos,
char and peel the peppers according to the recipe.
Then generously cut around and carefully pull out the
stems, setting them aside. Scrape out the seeds. Drain
the peppers, reserving any juice for the filling. Set the
bell peppers cut side up, stuff, and bake according to
the recipe. Position the reserved stem ends on top for
a fun presentation.

Tofu and Roasted Cheesy Tomato Scramble

SERVES 4

Tofu scramble makes for a delicious, wholesome breakfast. Turmeric gives the tofu its deep yellow color, a beautiful canvas for the cheesy herbed tomatoes. This recipe suggests plating the tofu for a quick-and-easy presentation, but you could also serve it in lettuce cups for added crunch and color.

4	large **sage leaves**, minced
2	**rosemary sprigs**, leaves minced
4	**thyme sprigs**, leaves only
4	ripe medium **tomatoes**, halved crosswise
¼–⅓	cup **olive oil**
	Kosher salt and freshly ground **black pepper**
3	large **garlic cloves**, thinly sliced
2	cups **grated Parmesan cheese**
1	**scallion**, root end and tough green top trimmed, white and green parts chopped
2	(14-ounce) containers **extra-firm regular tofu**, drained (page 7) and crumbled
½	teaspoon **turmeric powder**

1 Preheat the oven to 400°F (200°C). Line a baking pan with parchment paper.

2 Mix together the sage, rosemary, and thyme in a small bowl.

3 Place the tomatoes cut side up on the prepared baking pan. Drizzle them with 2 to 3 tablespoons of the oil and season with salt and pepper. Generously sprinkle each piece with the herb mixture, garlic, and Parmesan. Bake for about 25 minutes, until soft and golden.

4 Heat 2 tablespoons oil in a nonstick pan over medium-high heat. Add the scallion and sauté until just golden, about 3 minutes. Add the tofu and turmeric and stir until well combined. Season to taste with salt and pepper, and continue to cook until heated through, about 10 minutes.

5 Evenly divide the tofu among four individual plates, placing 2 roasted tomato halves on each serving.

Teriyaki Tofu

SERVES 4

True teriyaki sauce relies on a base of soy and sake. This version adds freshly squeezed ginger juice and scallion. This recipe yields 2 cups of teriyaki sauce, but you only need about ⅓ cup. Refrigerate the leftover sauce; it will keep for weeks. *Note:* True teriyaki sauce is not gloopy. It is only slightly thickened and, therefore, delicate—unlike many Japanese American restaurant versions.

1 cup **sake**

1 cup **mirin**

1 cup **soy sauce**

⅓ cup **sugar**

2 teaspoons **cornstarch** mixed with 2 teaspoons **water** (optional)

1 (2-inch) piece fresh **ginger**, peeled and grated

1 (14-ounce) container **regular** or **silken tofu**, any consistency, drained (page 7)

4 cups cooked **sushi rice** (white or brown, or a combination) or **udon noodles**

1 **scallion**, root end and tough green top trimmed, white and green parts thinly sliced, for garnish

Toasted sesame seeds, for garnish

1 Combine the sake, mirin, soy sauce, and sugar in a small saucepan over medium heat. Bring to a gentle boil, then reduce the heat to low and simmer until thickened, about 15 minutes. If you want a thicker sauce, whisk in the cornstarch slurry and cook for 1 minute longer. Remove from the heat.

2 Hold the grated ginger between your palms and thoroughly squeeze out the juice into a bowl. Stir the ginger juice into the teriyaki sauce.

3 Cut the tofu into roughly 1-inch cubes. Bring a pot of water to a gentle boil over medium heat. Reduce the heat to low and poach the tofu for 5 minutes. Drain thoroughly.

4 Spoon 1 cup of the rice into each of four shallow bowls, then top with the tofu. Drizzle a small amount of teriyaki sauce over each serving. Garnish with scallions and a sprinkling of sesame seeds.

Tofu Bibimbap

SERVES 4

Rice is the most important staple in Asian cuisine. In fact, a meal without it is no meal at all. An ingredient cooked in multiple ways, rice is served plain or as a base for various toppings or stir-fries. In this case, it is a base for vegetable toppings and tofu with a spicy Korean chili sauce. A colorful presentation is desirable, with bits of each ingredient arranged in separate piles and served atop individual servings of rice.

1 (14-ounce) container **extra-firm regular tofu**, drained (page 7)

⅓ cup **gochujang**

⅓ cup **honey**, **maple syrup**, or **agave nectar**

⅓ cup **rice vinegar**

½ cup **grapeseed** or **vegetable oil**

1 small to medium **zucchini**, thinly sliced into rounds

1 large **carrot**, peeled and shredded

2 cups **mung bean sprouts**

12 large fresh **shiitake mushrooms**, stems removed and caps julienned

1 pound **baby spinach**

5 teaspoons **toasted sesame oil**

Toasted sesame seeds

Kosher salt

4 cups cooked **sushi rice**

2 **scallions**, root ends and tough green tops trimmed, white and green parts thinly sliced, for garnish (optional)

1 Cut the tofu cake in half lengthwise, then cut each half lengthwise again. Flip the 4 rectangular slices flat onto your cutting board, then cut each rectangle in half lengthwise to make 8 sticks. Cut each stick in half crosswise, then halve crosswise again. You should have 32 nuggets (see page 8).

2 Whisk together the gochujang, honey, and vinegar in a small bowl until smooth. Cover with plastic wrap and set aside.

3 Heat 1 tablespoon of the grapeseed oil in a large nonstick skillet over medium heat. Add the zucchini and stir-fry until softened, about 2 minutes, and transfer to a bowl. Replenishing the pan with 1 tablespoon grapeseed oil each time, stir-fry the following vegetables separately until softened, transferring each cooked vegetable to its own bowl: carrot, sprouts, and mushrooms for 2 minutes each, and spinach for 30 seconds. Top each vegetable with 1 teaspoon of the sesame oil, a light sprinkling of toasted sesame seeds, and a bit of salt, then toss to coat.

4 Rinse the skillet under hot running water and wipe clean. Heat the remaining 3 tablespoons grapeseed oil over medium-high heat and panfry the tofu cubes until golden, 1 to 2 minutes per side.

5 To assemble the bibimbap, spread 1 cup of rice across the bottom of each of four shallow bowls. Arrange the tofu, zucchini, carrot, sprouts, spinach, and mushrooms over the rice. Drizzle each serving with 3 tablespoons of the sauce, or according to taste. Garnish with scallions, if using.

Tofu Jambalaya

SERVES 8

Combine French, Spanish, and West African culinary influences and you get jambalaya. Originating in New Orleans, where Creole flavors permeate the local food scene, this rice dish is filling and rich with spices. Long-grain rice is a key ingredient because its grains separate nicely, in contrast to its short-grain cousin, which clumps.

The level of spiciness is up to you, but be sure not to skimp on herbs. The jambalaya consistency should be wet but not soupy, and the rice grains cooked but not mushy.

1 (14-ounce) container **extra-firm regular tofu**, drained (page 7)

¼ cup **olive oil**

1 large **onion**, chopped

2 large **garlic cloves**, chopped

2 **celery stalks**, peeled and chopped

1 medium **red bell pepper**, halved, stem and seeds removed, and chopped

1 medium **green bell pepper**, halved, stem and seeds removed, and chopped

1½ cups **long-grain rice**, rinsed until the water runs clear

2⅓ cups **vegetable stock**

1 (28-ounce) can crushed **tomatoes**

4 **thyme sprigs**, leaves only

4 **oregano sprigs**, leaves only

4 **basil sprigs**, leaves freshly torn

2 teaspoons **smoked paprika**

½ teaspoon **cayenne pepper**

Kosher salt and freshly ground **black pepper**

8 pieces **okra**, stems removed, cut into ¼-inch slices

1 Cut the tofu cake in half lengthwise, then cut each half lengthwise again. Flip the 4 rectangular slices flat onto your cutting board, then cut each rectangle in half lengthwise to make 8 sticks. Cut each stick in half crosswise, then halve crosswise again. You should have 32 nuggets (see page 8).

2 Heat the oil in a medium pot over medium heat. Add the onion and garlic and cook until browned, about 5 minutes. Add the celery and bell peppers and cook until softened and fragrant, about 10 minutes.

3 Stir in the rice, stock, tomatoes, thyme, oregano, basil, smoked paprika, and cayenne. Season to taste with salt and black pepper, reduce the heat to low, cover, and cook until the rice is done, about 20 minutes.

4 Add the tofu and okra, stirring gently until well incorporated in the stew, and cook until the okra is tender, about 10 minutes. Serve warm.

Tofu Katsu
with Kare Sauce

SERVES 4

Japanese kare (curry) is unique among Asian curries in that it starts with a roux. Classic ingredients include potatoes, carrots, peas, and some sort of protein stewed in a thick curry sauce and served over rice. A comfort food, Japanese curry pleases young and adult palates alike. Here the tofu is dipped in egg wash, then coated with panko and oven-crisped.

¼ cup **grapeseed** or **vegetable oil**

1 medium **onion**, finely chopped

1 (1-inch) piece fresh **ginger**, peeled and finely grated

1 large **garlic clove**, minced

1 small sweet **apple**, such as Fuji or Gala, peeled, halved, cored, and grated

3 tablespoons **all-purpose flour**

3 tablespoons **curry powder**

1 tablespoon **tomato paste** (optional)

3 cups low-sodium or salt-free **vegetable stock**

1 cup **sake**

2 tablespoons **soy sauce**

Cayenne pepper (optional)

1 large **carrot**, peeled and cut into ½-inch cubes

1 large **waxy potato**, peeled and cut into ¾-inch cubes

8 baby bella or button **mushrooms**, stems trimmed, caps quartered

½ cup frozen **peas**

2 **eggs**

2 cups **panko**

2 (14-ounce) containers **firm regular tofu**, drained (page 7)

4 cups cooked **sushi rice** (white or brown, or a combination) or **udon noodles**

1 Heat 3 tablespoons of the oil in a medium pot over medium heat. Stir in the onion, ginger, and garlic, and sauté until lightly browned, about 5 minutes. Stir in the apple and cook until lightly caramelized, about 3 minutes. Stir in the flour and cook until thickened. Stir in the curry powder and toast for 1 minute. Stir in the tomato paste, if using, then add the stock, sake, soy sauce, and cayenne, if using. Add the carrot, potato, and mushrooms. Reduce the heat to medium-low. Partially cover and gently boil, stirring occasionally, until thickened to a loose custard consistency (not too thin and not too thick), 30 to 45 minutes. Add the peas and cook for 5 minutes longer.

2 Preheat the oven to 400°F (200°C). Line a baking pan with parchment paper.

3 Whisk the eggs in a wide shallow bowl. Toss the panko with the remaining 1 tablespoon oil in a separate shallow bowl.

4 Cut each tofu cake crosswise into 8 equal slices, for a total of 16 pieces. Dip each piece of tofu in the egg wash, then coat on all sides with the panko mixture and place on the prepared baking pan. Bake for about 20 minutes, flipping once, until browned.

5 Spoon 1 cup of the rice into one side of each of four shallow bowls. Ladle a portion of vegetable curry next to the rice, then top the rice with 4 pieces of tofu katsu.

6

Sweets

Silken tofu is particularly well suited for desserts and other sweet foods. Creamy and rich, it replaces yogurt nicely and enhances flavors with an earthy note. It also absorbs flavor effortlessly. A single bite of any of these treats will satisfy your sweet tooth and counter-balance the natural bitter and tangy characteristics of tea or coffee.

Tofu Oatmeal-Banana-Walnut Pancakes

SERVES 4

For a wholesome breakfast with leftovers to snack on, make plenty of these pancakes and reheat them in the oven or toast them the next day. Any fruit works for the topping; use whatever fruit is in season for the best results.

1   (12-ounce) container **silken tofu**

½   cup unsweetened **soy milk, almond milk, or oat milk**

1   tablespoon **vanilla extract**

1   ripe **banana**

2   **eggs**

2   cups **quick-cooking oats**

2   teaspoons **baking powder**

½   teaspoon **kosher salt**

½   cup crushed raw **walnuts**

Coconut oil

2   cups fresh **berries**

Butter or **nut butter** of choice, for serving

Maple syrup, for serving

1   Place the tofu, soy milk, vanilla, banana, eggs, oats, baking powder, and salt in a food processor. Process until smooth. Pour into a bowl and stir in the walnuts.

2   Cooking in batches, heat 1 to 2 teaspoons of the oil in a large nonstick skillet or on a griddle over medium heat. Ladle the batter into the pan (⅓ cup of batter per pancake), fitting in as many pancakes as the pan will hold (in general, 2 to 4 pancakes depending on the size of the pan). Cook until golden on the bottom and bubbly on top, about 2 minutes. Flip the pancakes and cook until golden on the other side, 1 to 2 minutes longer. Repeat until you've used all the batter.

3   Serve the pancakes hot, with the fresh berries, butter, and maple syrup on the side.

Tofu-Mango Lassi

SERVES 4

Traditionally made with fresh yogurt, this Indian-inspired mango lassi is rich with cardamom and made using soft silken tofu, resulting in a smooth texture and earthy flavor. My suggestion is to taste the fruit and add sweetener accordingly. Though salt may not be traditionally used in lassi, a pinch will offset the sweetness of the beverage and round out the flavors.

2 cups ripe fresh or frozen **mango** pieces

1 (12-ounce) container **silken tofu**, chilled

½ teaspoon **ground cardamom**

½–1 cup unsweetened **soy milk**, chilled (see Tips)

Agave nectar, **light honey**, or **maple syrup** (see Tips)

Pinch of **kosher salt**

Place the mango, tofu, and cardamom in a blender. Process, then add ½ cup of the soy milk and process again. Add more milk as needed. Look for a consistency similar to loose custard or slightly thinner. Taste the lassi and sweeten as desired. Add the salt and process one more time.

TIPS | You can adjust the amount of soy milk according to the consistency you prefer.

Frozen mango is rarely sweet. If you're using it, adjust the sweetness to taste by gradually adding agave nectar, light honey, or maple syrup.

Tofu Banana Chocolate Pudding

SERVES 4

Chocolate pudding is easy to make; you can use white, milk, or dark chocolate morsels to create your favorite version. This version uses dark chocolate for its subtle bitter note and to counterbalance an otherwise sweet dessert.

½ cup **soy milk**, warmed

1 cup bittersweet **chocolate chips**, melted

2 (12-ounce) containers **silken tofu**

1 large ripe **banana**, chopped

Maldon sea salt flakes, for garnish

Combine the warm soy milk and melted chocolate chips in a blender and process until smooth. Add the tofu and banana and process until smooth. Spoon evenly into four individual dessert bowls and chill for 30 minutes. Serve, garnished lightly with salt.

TIP | Rely on the natural sweetness of the banana. If you like chocolate pudding on the sweet side, gradually add agave nectar or maple syrup, 1 tablespoon at a time, or simply use milk chocolate chips in the recipe instead. In general, the lighter the chocolate, the creamier and sweeter the pudding will be.

Tofu Almond Matcha Fool

SERVES 4

This fool is a colorful dessert, and its layers should be shown through glass. Use small-stem glassware or clear ramekins to show off your creations. The number of layers will be determined by the shape of the vessel. For instance, a long and slender champagne glass will need about four layers, while a small wine glass will likely require three. Use any glass you have and have fun with the layering. Matcha goes a long way—dust lightly!

2 tablespoons **coconut oil**, plus more for greasing

¼ cup **sugar**

1 cup crushed plain **dry-roasted almonds**

Pinch of **kosher salt**

1 (12-ounce) container **firm silken tofu**

¼ cup **maple syrup**

1 tablespoon **vanilla extract**

½ cup **puffed wheat** or **puffed rice cereal** or plain **granola**

Matcha powder, for garnish

1 Lightly grease a nonstick baking pan.

2 Warm the coconut oil and sugar in a skillet over medium-low heat. Stir until well combined, browned, and reduced, 3 to 5 minutes. Add the almonds and salt and stir to coat well. Spread over the prepared baking pan. Set aside to cool. Once it's cooled, crush the brittle and transfer to a bowl.

3 Combine the tofu, maple syrup, and vanilla in a blender. Process until smooth. Refrigerate the tofu custard for 1 hour.

4 Place 2 tablespoons cereal in each of four small glass containers. Top with ¼ cup plus 2 tablespoons tofu custard. Garnish with 2 heaping tablespoons almond brittle. Put some matcha powder in a fine-mesh sieve and lightly dust the top of each serving.

Tofu Mocha Brownies

MAKES 16 PIECES OR 8 SLICES

Everyone likes a good brownie, and silken tofu makes for a perfectly pillowy consistency. Enjoy these brownies as is or with walnuts for added texture. For fun, these brownies can be baked in a round fluted tart pan, sliced into wedges, and served warm with vanilla ice cream.

- 2 tablespoons **grapeseed** or **vegetable oil**, plus more for greasing
- 1 (12-ounce) container **silken tofu**
- ¼ cup **agave nectar**
- ½ cup strong **coffee**
- 1 tablespoon **vanilla extract**
- 1¼ cups **all-purpose flour**
- ½ cup unsweetened **cocoa powder**
- ½ cup **sugar**
- 1 teaspoon **baking powder**
- ½ teaspoon **kosher salt**
- ½ cup chopped **walnuts** (optional)

1 Preheat the oven to 350°F (180°C). Thoroughly grease a rectangular nonstick baking dish or round fluted tart pan.

2 Place the oil, tofu, agave nectar, coffee, vanilla, flour, cocoa, sugar, baking powder, and salt in a food processor. Process until smooth. (If using the nuts, transfer the batter to a mixing bowl and fold in the nuts now.)

3 Scrape the batter into the prepared baking dish. Bake for about 35 minutes, until a toothpick inserted in the center comes out clean. Cool for 20 minutes before removing from the baking dish and slicing.

Tofu Pineapple-Coconut-Rum Custard

SERVES 4

Cool, rich, almost like ice cream but lighter, this silken tofu piña colada–style custard is the perfect chilled summertime dessert. The key to a naturally sweet custard is to choose super-ripe pineapple.

1 small ripe **pineapple**, peeled, cored, and cut into chunks

1 (12-ounce) container **silken tofu**

½ cup unsweetened **coconut cream** (see Tip)

2 tablespoons **rum**

2 teaspoons **cornstarch**

1 tablespoon **agave nectar** (optional)

1⅓ cups low-sugar **granola**

4 tablespoons plain roasted **slivered almonds**, for garnish

1 Place the pineapple chunks in a food processor and process until smooth. Push the purée through a fine-mesh sieve, pressing to extract as much of the pulp as possible. Discard the fibrous mass.

2 Return the pineapple purée to the food processor. Add the tofu, coconut cream, rum, and cornstarch. Process until smooth and thick. Taste; stir in the agave nectar gradually and only if necessary. Refrigerate the custard for 1 hour.

3 Spoon ⅓ cup granola into each of four small wine glasses. Divide the custard into 4 equal portions and spoon it on top of the granola. Garnish each serving with 1 tablespoon of the almonds.

TIP | Coconut cream is thick and generally rises to the top of a can of coconut milk. Do not shake the can before opening it! Spoon off the cream and reserve the liquid milk for another recipe, such as Tofu-Mango Lassi (page 109).

Bumbleberry Tofu Custard

SERVES 4

Mixed berries—a.k.a. bumbleberry—make for a great balance of sweet and tangy notes. Including blackberries will give the custard a beautiful deep purple color. When using fresh berries, make sure they are very ripe so that this recipe shines.

2   (12-ounce) containers **silken tofu**

½   cup fresh or frozen **blackberries**

½   cup fresh or frozen **blueberries**

½   cup fresh or frozen **raspberries**

½   cup fresh or frozen **strawberries**

    Agave nectar (optional)

8   **mint leaves**, finely julienned

Place the tofu, blackberries, blueberries, raspberries, and strawberries in a food processor. Process until smooth. Taste the custard; if it needs sweetening, add 1 tablespoon of agave nectar at a time, then process again. Serve in individual bowls, garnished with mint.

ESSENTIAL INGREDIENTS

While all of the ingredients featured in this book are readily available, some may be more familiar than others. For the sake of facilitating your cooking experience, here is a quick overview of some of the ingredients you will find in the international aisle of your local supermarket or in Asian or health food stores. Rest assured that you will have no trouble locating them.

AGAVE NECTAR. This syrup is made from the sap of the agave plant, also used in making tequila. A sugar substitute, though sweeter (less is more), and easy to incorporate into sauces, it is a great alternative to honey for vegan cuisine.

BLACK BEAN AND GARLIC SAUCE. Ready-made and store-bought, this sauce is made from oxidized salted soybeans and garlic, incorporating wheat for fermenting, and salt, sugar, and rice wine for preserving. Some brands include ginger.

CHIPOTLE CHILES IN ADOBO SAUCE. These are smoked and spicy hot jalapeños preserved in tomato sauce and spices and widely used in Mexican and Tex-Mex cooking. Like all chiles, the heat from the jalapeño comes mostly from the seeds; removing them prior to cooking with the chile will tame the heat.

CURRY PASTE. Red or green Thai curry paste contains chiles, lemongrass, garlic, galangal, and other spices. Some brands are spicier or saltier than others. Be sure to adjust the seasoning in the recipes accordingly.

CURRY POWDER. This dried spice blend includes chiles, turmeric, coriander, cumin, cinnamon, ginger, garlic, fenugreek, and so much more. Some are spicy while others are mild. Each brand has its own recipe, but they are all close enough in formula. Feel free to use your favorite brand.

DAIKON. A long and thick white radish used widely in Asian cooking; as an alternative, use any large common radish.

DIJON MUSTARD. Made from mustard seeds, white vinegar, white wine, and allspice, both mild and hot versions of this mustard come from the city of Dijon in Burgundy, France. This classic condiment is also available as a grainy mustard.

DRIED SHIITAKE MUSHROOMS. Unlike the mildly flavored, delicate, and tender fresh shiitakes sold in the produce section, the dried versions are very fragrant and somewhat chewy. Find them in the international or organic aisle of supermarkets, and in Asian and health food stores.

EDAMAME. Sold in the frozen section, in the pod or shelled, these are young green soybeans that are tender yet firm. Steamed or blanched, these are often served in Japanese restaurants sprinkled with salt, a recipe easily replicated at home. Additionally, edamame are delicious added to soups, stir-fries, or salads. They can also be incorporated into creamy dips.

FISH SAUCE. This condiment is made from anchovies layered with salt, topped with water, and left to ferment in barrels for months prior to extracting the liquid, which is then bottled. Though used as salt in Southeast Asian cuisines, the sauce provides a distinct flavor. Purchase in small bottles or according to your personal consumption. Refrigerate after opening to maintain optimal flavor for up to 9 months, after which the sauce should be replaced. Look for a golden amber color. Fish sauce darkens over time, becoming as dark as coffee. Once salt crystals form at the bottom of the bottle, the sauce has passed its prime and is increasingly salty, with its fish essence muddied.

FIVE-SPICE POWDER. Often containing more than five spices, the common blend combines star anise, cinnamon, fennel, cloves, and Szechuan peppercorns. Some combinations include dried ginger and dried mandarin peel, among other spices. The "five" in five-spice refers to nature's elements of water, earth, fire, wood, and metal, not the actual number of spices.

GOCHUJANG. Made from chiles, glutinous (sticky) rice, malt, and salt, this is a fermented sweet, savory, and hot paste widely used in Korean cuisine. Versatile, it is increasingly used in contemporary recipes as a chili sauce alternative and incorporated into marinades and dipping sauces.

GRAPESEED OIL. A cooking oil that has the same health benefits as olive oil but can be used for high-temperature cooking such as stir-frying. A by-product of winemaking, it is derived from grape seeds.

HOISIN SAUCE. A soybean-based product, hoisin sauce is made with vinegar, garlic, sesame oil, sugar, and salt. Because it is thick, it is used in marinades, often in combination with soy sauce and sugar.

KELP. Also known as kombu, kelp is an edible seaweed used for deepening the flavor of stocks and sauces. Widely used in Japanese cuisine for over a thousand years, it can be found in Asian and health food stores.

LEMONGRASS. Technically a grass, it is also known as citronella and has a distinct citrus note resembling that of lemon. Depending on its culinary use, it can be crushed, sliced, or grated.

LIQUID AMINOS. This gluten-free, unfermented, soybean-based condiment can be used as a soup base, a seasoning for stir-fries, or an ingredient in marinade. It's a seasoning much like soy sauce, but with a distinct flavor. A second type exists that is coconut based and very different in flavor. The one called for in this book is the soy-based version.

MIRIN. Made from fermented rice, mirin is a sweet sake used in Japanese cooking. Different grades exist; the top one is made from a base that is 100 percent rice, and its sweetness comes entirely from the fermentation process. It has a higher alcohol content than the mirin sold for cooking (which is often sweetened artificially). This condiment deepens the flavor of marinades, sauces, and salad dressings, counterbalancing their otherwise salty characteristic.

NORI. An edible seaweed sold in very thin, flat black sheets and used to wrap rice-based foods such as Japanese sushi, hand rolls, onigiri, and Korean kimbap, nori is savory, flaky when dry, and slightly chewy when moistened. It is also sold as flakes to sprinkle over rice or noodle dishes.

NUTRITIONAL YEAST. An inactive yeast sold in powder or granulated form, it is added to vegan dishes as a cheese substitute. It also acts as a binding and thickening agent.

PICKLED GINGER. Young ginger that has been pickled with sugar, salt, and rice vinegar, this is sold ready-made, plain or pink from red food coloring, and thinly sliced or shredded.

RICE PAPER. Made from a combination of rice and tapioca flour, salt, and water, rice paper sheets must be dipped in water to rehydrate before they can be used for rolling.

RICE VERMICELLI. Made from rice flour that has been shaped and dried into thin strands resembling angel hair pasta in thickness, rice vermicelli is far more delicate and quick-cooking than Italian wheat-based vermicelli. These fragile rice noodles require only 10 seconds to cook.

HOMEMADE MIRIN

It's easy to make your own mirin. Heat ½ cup sugar in a pan over medium heat until bubbly and light golden, 2 to 3 minutes. In a steady stream, stir in 1 cup sake, and simmer until reduced and slightly thickened like simple syrup.

RICE VINEGAR. This mildly flavored condiment is made from fermented rice. Two types are sold: unseasoned, which is preferred for cooking (and listed in the ingredients as simply "rice vinegar"), and seasoned, used for making sushi (or pickled) rice. The only substitute is white vinegar diluted with some water.

SAKE. There are many qualities of this Japanese rice wine, with prices to match. Use an inexpensive, though drinkable, type for cooking.

SAMBAL OELEK. This chunky raw hot chili sauce, made with red chiles, vinegar, and salt, is readily available in Asian markets and occasionally found in the international aisle of supermarkets.

SHICHIMI TOGARASHI. A flavorful Japanese chili powder mix, often including sesame seeds, orange peel, ginger, shiso, and more, it can be sprinkled on all sorts of rice and noodle dishes.

SHIRO MISO. Also known as white miso, this fermented soybean paste is made purely from soybeans, salt, and koji, a fungus. Shiro miso is the key ingredient for making the popular miso soup. While there are dozens of different types of miso pastes, they are derived from three basic versions: white, red, and black. The darker the miso, the saltier it is. Shiro miso is beige in color and can be found in the refrigerated section of your local supermarket. Some brands include rice or wheat as fermenting agents.

SRIRACHA SAUCE. A smooth, thick hot sauce made from cayenne peppers, garlic, vinegar, sugar, and salt. A Southeast Asian condiment associated with Thai and Vietnamese cuisines, it is also produced in the United States and widely used in home kitchens and restaurants alike. Sriracha is mixed with mayonnaise to make the popular spicy tuna rolls in Japanese sushi restaurants.

SUSHI RICE. A short-grain rice of the Japonica variety. When cooked, it offers a combination of textures, including soft, chewy, and sticky, all in the same bite. Readily available, the best quality comes from Japan, though California-grown sushi rice is also good, with slightly bigger grains that are considered "medium."

TAHINI. A 100 percent pure sesame paste made from hulled or unhulled, raw or roasted seeds, with or without salt, tahini is a condiment used in Middle Eastern cooking. Naturally bitter, it is often mixed with other ingredients such as lemon juice and salt to tame its flavor. It is also a common ingredient in hummus. Available in health food stores and sometimes found in the international aisle of supermarkets.

TAPIOCA STARCH. A flavorless thickening agent derived from the cassava root, also known as yuca and manioc; use cornstarch as a substitute.

THAI CHILES. Rated at about 8 of 10 on the Scoville heat scale, these tiny chiles are available in red or green and measure 1 to 1½ inches long. Substitute one-quarter to one-third of a Scotch bonnet or one to two jalapeños for every Thai chile. As with all chiles, the heat comes mostly from the seeds; removing them prior to cooking with the chiles will tame the heat.

TOASTED SESAME OIL. Also known as dark sesame oil or roasted sesame oil, this dark, very fragrant finishing or flavoring oil is best applied to a dish at the last minute or integrated into marinades or salad dressing. Like many nut oils or delicate oils, sesame oil will burn at high temperature. For this reason, do not stir-fry with it. Instead, as you are taking food off the heat, drizzle on a small amount of toasted sesame oil and toss quickly. A small amount will go a long way.

TURMERIC POWDER. Made from the turmeric rhizome, it has an earthy note and is the base ingredient in Indian curry powder. With its bright yellow color, it is often used for coloring foods.

UDON. A wheat-based thick Japanese noodle with Chinese origins, udon or thick wheat noodles can be found in Asian and health food stores and international aisles of supermarkets.

WAKAME. An edible seaweed added to miso soup or salads, it can be found in Asian or Japanese stores, as well as the international or health food aisle of supermarkets.

WASABI. This root, when freshly grated, resembles horseradish in intensity and flavor. It is most available in powder form or as a paste sold in tubes. Use two parts powder to one part water to make a paste.

WONTON WRAPPERS. Sold in the refrigerated (and frozen) section in grocery stores, often next to tofu at the far end of a produce aisle, wonton wrappers are typically round or square. Some are thinner than others, but all can be used for making dumplings.

METRIC CONVERSION CHART

To convert	To	Multiply
teaspoons	milliliters	teaspoons by 4.93
tablespoons	milliliters	tablespoons by 14.79
fluid ounces	milliliters	fluid ounces by 29.57
cups	milliliters	cups by 236.59
cups	liters	cups by 0.24
pints	milliliters	pints by 473.18
pints	liters	pints by 0.473
quarts	milliliters	quarts by 946.36
quarts	liters	quarts by 0.946
gallons	liters	gallons by 3.785

ACKNOWLEDGMENTS

Conceptualizing, writing, and otherwise developing a book requires a great team with a good amount of synergy. While I was working on multiple projects across the oceans, it took a small village to create the beautiful pages and delicious recipes you now get to enjoy.

I want to thank that small village for their contribution, sharp eyes and curious minds, and professionalism and enthusiasm.

To acquiring editor Deanna Cook, for giving me the chance to put tofu on the table for good, demystifying this soybean product for fans and skeptics alike, thank you.

Everyone needs an editor. I had a few, and all were tasked with different jobs. A huge thank-you to project editor Sarah Guare Slattery for staying on top of the details and carrying this project to fruition. Thanks also to copy editor Paula Brisco for her expertise with grammar, punctuation, and syntax—all the things we can easily skip over as writers, especially when we're "in flow." Thank you to proofreaders Nancy Ringer and Alissa Cyphers for dotting the i's and crossing the t's, and indexer Andrea Chesman for helping readers navigate the pages effortlessly. And what's a cookbook without enticing photographs? To photographer Kate Sears and food stylist Liza Jernow, thank you for making food look so good on paper; I can taste it. Finally, thanks to art director Ash Austin and production designer Slavica Walzl for the colorful design that makes words, colors, and pictures dance on each page in an elegant and user-friendly way.

For 14 years, Beth Shepard has been my agent and one of the sharpest sounding boards I've ever had the pleasure of working with. Thank you again for sticking by me.

To my parents, Marie-Jeanne "Minou" Trang and Nhu Minh Trang, and the rest of the Trang clan, a rather large family of food enthusiasts and incredible home cooks and chefs: You are the foundation upon which my palate has developed over decades while growing on three different continents and traveling the world, eating my way through home kitchens, restaurants, and street food markets, with an open mind and heart.

Always a pleasure,

INDEX

Page numbers in *italic* are photographs.

ENJOY FLAVOR-PACKED MEALS
with More Books from Storey

by Nicki Sizemore

Discover the versatility of bowl meals with this collection of 77 delicious, nutrition-packed recipes featuring grains, legumes, vegetables, poultry, seafood, and more. Countless customizing options help you suit individual diets and tastes.

by Unmi Abkin and Roger Taylor

Two award-winning chefs share their most acclaimed recipes along with the foundational dressings, salsas, broths, and infused oils that are the key to delivering outstanding flavor. Favorites include a Korean-inspired Bolognese sauce for Korean Sloppy Joes, Chow Fun Sauce for Coriander Shrimp Chow Fun, Scallion Ginger Jam for Clay Pot Miso Chicken, and Ponzu Sauce for Miso-Glazed Cod Rice Bowl.

by Kirsten K. Shockey and Christopher Shockey

Master the techniques for making sauerkraut, kimchi, pickles, and other savory, probiotic-rich foods in your own kitchen. This best-selling, easy-to-follow guide offers more than 120 recipes for fermenting 64 different vegetables and herbs.